THIS BOOK BELONGS TO:

Declan McGoigan.

with love from your wee Mammy xxx

IF FOUND PLEASE CONTACT:

© 2022 Saltire Publishing. All rights reserved.

RANK	PAGE #	MUNRO	ALTITUDE	HIKED
1	58	Ben Nevis (Beinn Nibheis)	1,344.53M	☐
2	18	Ben Macdui (Beinn Macduibh)	1,309M	☐
3	15	Braeriach (Am Bràigh Riabhach)	1,296M	☐
4	1	Cairn Toul (Càrn an t-Sabhail)	1,291M	☐
5	2	Sgor an Lochain Uaine	1,258M	☐
6	231	Cairn Gorm (An Càrn Gorm)	1,244.80M	☐
7	59	Aonach Beag	1,234M	☐
8	60	Aonach Mòr	1,220.40M	☐
9	61	Càrn Mòr Dearg	1,220M	☐
10	238	Ben Lawers (Beinn Labhair)	1,214M	☐
11	19	Beinn a' Bhùird	1,197M	☐
12	237	Beinn Mheadhoin	1,182.90M	☐
13	62	Càrn Eige	1,182.80M	☐
14	63	Mam Sodhail	1,179.40M	☐
15	64	Stob Choire Claurigh	1,177M	☐
16	269	Ben More (A' Bheinn Mhòr)	1,174M	☐
17	20	Ben Avon (Beinn Athfhinn)	1,172M	☐
18	270	Stob Binnein	1,165M	☐
19	3	Beinn Bhrotain	1,157M	☐
20	4	Lochnagar (Beinn Chìochan)	1,155.70M	☐
21	5	Derry Cairngorm (Càrn Gorm an Doire)	1,155M	☐
22	65	Sgurr nan Ceathreamhnan	1,151M	☐
23	66	Sgurr na Lapaich	1,151M	☐
24	67	Bidean nam Bian	1,149.40M	☐
25	68	Ben Alder (Beinn Eallair)	1,148M	☐
26	69	Geal-Chàrn	1,132M	☐
27	271	Ben Lui (Beinn Laoigh)	1,131.40M	☐
28	70	Binnein Mòr	1,130M	☐
29	71	An Riabhachan	1,129M	☐
30	72	Creag Meagaidh	1,128.10M	☐
31	36	Ben Cruachan	1,127M	☐
32	239	Meall Garbh	1,123.10M	☐
33	240	Beinn a' Ghló - Càrn nan Gabhar	1,121.90M	☐
34	73	A' Chraileag (A' Chràlaig)	1,120M	☐
35	74	Sgor Gaoith	1,118M	☐
36	241	An Stuc	1,117.10M	☐
37	75	Stob Coire an Laoigh	1,116M	☐
38	76	Aonach Beag	1,115.80M	☐
39	77	Stob Coire Easain	1,115M	☐
40	16	Monadh Mòr	1,113M	☐
41	78	Tom a' Choinich	1,112M	☐
42	6	Càrn a' Choire Bhoidheach	1,109.90M	☐
43	79	Sgurr nan Conbhairean	1,109M	☐
44	80	Sgurr Mòr	1,108.90M	☐
45	81	Meall a' Bhuiridh	1,107.90M	☐
46	82	Stob a' Choire Mheadhoin	1,105M	☐
47	83	Beinn Eibhinn	1,103.30M	☐
48	242	Beinn Ghlas	1,103M	☐
49	84	Mullach Fraoch-choire	1,102M	☐

RANK	PAGE #	MUNRO	ALTITUDE	HIKED
50	85	Creise	1,099.30M	☐
51	86	Sgurr a' Mhaim	1,099M	☐
52	87	Sgurr Choinnich Mòr	1,094M	☐
53	88	Sgurr nan Clach Geala	1,093M	☐
54	52	Stob Ghabhar	1,090M	☐
55	89	Bynack More	1,090M	☐
56	90	Beinn a' Chlachair	1,087M	☐
57	91	Beinn Dearg	1,084M	☐
58	92	Sgurr a' Choire Ghlais	1,083M	☐
59	243	Schiehallion (Sìdh Chailleann)	1,083M	☐
60	21	Beinn a' Chaorainn	1,083M	☐
61	244	Beinn a' Chreachain	1,080.60M	☐
62	93	Ben Starav	1,079.50M	☐
63	245	Beinn Heasgarnich	1,077.40M	☐
64	37	Beinn Dorain	1,076M	☐
65	94	Bidean nam Bian - Stob Coire Sgreamhach	1,072M	☐
66	246	Beinn a' Ghlò - Bràigh Coire Chruinn-bhalgain	1,070M	☐
67	95	An Socach	1,069M	☐
68	247	Meall Corranaich	1,069M	☐
69	96	Sgurr Fhuaran	1,068.80M	☐
70	31	Glas Maol	1,068M	☐
71	26	Cairn of Claise	1,064M	☐
72	97	An Teallach - Bidein a' Ghlas Thuill	1,062.50M	☐
73	98	An Teallach - Sgurr Fiona	1,058.70M	☐
74	99	Liathach - Spidean a' Choire Lèith	1,054.80M	☐
75	100	Na Gruagaichean	1,054.30M	☐
76	101	Toll Creagach	1,054M	☐
77	102	Stob Poite Coire Ardair	1,054M	☐
78	103	Sgurr a' Chaorachain	1,053M	☐
79	248	Glas Tulaichean	1,051M	☐
80	104	Beinn a' Chaorainn	1,049.10M	☐
81	105	Geal Charn	1,049M	☐
82	106	Sgurr Fhuar-thuill	1,049M	☐
83	7	Càrn an t-Sagairt Mòr	1,047M	☐
84	266	Creag Mhòr	1,046.80M	☐
85	107	Ben Wyvis	1,046M	☐
86	108	Chno Dearg	1,046M	☐
87	272	Cruach Ardrain	1,045.90M	☐
88	22	Beinn Iutharn Mhòr	1,045M	☐
89	53	Stob Coir'an Albannaich	1,044M	☐
90	249	Meall nan Tarmachan	1,043.60M	☐
91	250	Càrn Mairg	1,042M	☐
92	109	Sgùrr na Cìche	1,040.20M	☐
93	267	Meall Ghaordaidh	1,039.80M	☐
94	56	Beinn Achaladair	1,038.60M	☐
95	8	Càrn a' Mhaim	1,037M	☐
96	110	Sgurr a' Bhealaich Dheirg	1,036M	☐
97	111	Gleouraich	1,035M	☐
98	112	Càrn Dearg	1,034M	☐

RANK	PAGE #	MUNRO	ALTITUDE	HIKED
99	113	Beinn Fhada (Ben Attow)	1,031.90m	☐
100	114	Am Bodach	1,031.80m	☐
101	273	Ben Oss	1,029m	☐
102	251	Càrn an Rìgh	1,029m	☐
103	252	Càrn Gorm	1,029m	☐
104	115	Sgurr a' Mhaoraich	1,027m	☐
105	116	Sgurr na Ciste Duibhe	1,027m	☐
106	274	Beinn Challuim (Ben Challum)	1,025m	☐
107	117	Beinn a' Bheithir - Sgorr Dhearg	1,024m	☐
108	118	Liathach - Mullach an Rathain	1,023.80m	☐
109	119	Buachaille Etive Mòr - Stob Dearg	1,021.40m	☐
110	120	Ladhar Bheinn	1,020m	☐
111	121	Aonach air Chrith	1,019.50m	☐
112	122	Beinn Bheoil	1,019m	☐
113	123	Mullach Clach a' Bhlair	1,019m	☐
114	9	Càrn an Tuirc	1,019m	☐
115	124	Mullach Coire Mhic Fhearchair	1,015.20m	☐
116	125	Garbh Chioch Mhòr	1,012.90m	☐
117	38	Beinn Ìme	1,012.20m	☐
118	27	Cairn Bannoch	1,012m	☐
119	126	The Saddle (An Dìollaid)	1,011.50m	☐
120	232	Beinn Udlamain	1,010.20m	☐
121	127	Beinn Eighe - Ruadh-stac Mòr	1,010m	☐
122	128	Sgurr Eilde Mòr	1,010m	☐
123	129	Sgurr an Doire Leathain	1,010m	☐
124	253	Beinn Dearg	1,008.70m	☐
125	10	The Devil's Point	1,006.90m	☐
126	23	An Sgarsoch	1,006.50m	☐
127	130	Càrn Liath	1,006m	☐
128	131	Maoile Lunndaidh	1,004.90m	☐
129	132	Beinn Fhionnlaidh	1,004.80m	☐
130	39	Beinn an Dothaidh	1,004m	☐
131	133	Sgurr an Lochain	1,004m	☐
132	134	Sgurr Mor	1,003m	☐
133	135	Sgurr na Carnach	1,002m	☐
134	136	Beinn a' Bheithir - Sgorr Dhonuill	1,001m	☐
135	137	Aonach Meadhoin	1,001m	☐
136	254	Meall Greigh	1,001m	☐
137	138	Stob Bàn	999.7m	☐
138	139	Sgurr Breac	999.6m	☐
139	140	Sgurr Choinnich	999.3m	☐
140	40	Stob Daimh	999.2m	☐
141	141	Sail Chaorainn	999.2m	☐
142	142	A' Chailleach	998.6m	☐
143	143	Ben More Assynt	998m	☐
144	28	Broad Cairn	998m	☐
145	54	Glas Bheinn Mhòr	997.7m	☐
146	144	Spidean Mialach	996m	☐
147	275	An Caisteal	995.9m	☐

RANK	PAGE #	MUNRO	ALTITUDE	HIKED
148	145	Sgurr na h-Ulaidh	994m	☐
149	17	Carn an Fhidhleir	994m	☐
150	146	Sgurr na Ruaidhe	993m	☐
151	147	Càrn nan Gobhar (Mullardoch)	993m	☐
152	148	Beinn Eighe - Spidean Coire nan Clach	993m	☐
153	149	Sgùrr Alasdair	992m	☐
154	150	Càrn nan Gobhar (Strathfarrar)	992m	☐
155	255	Sgairneach Mhòr	991m	☐
156	41	Beinn Eunaich	989m	☐
157	151	Sgurr Bàn	989m	☐
158	35	Creag Leacach	988.2m	☐
159	152	Gaor Bheinn (Gulvain)	987m	☐
160	153	Lurg Mhòr	987m	☐
161	154	Conival	987m	☐
162	155	Beinn Alligin - Sgùrr Mhòr	986m	☐
163	156	Sgùrr Dearg (Inaccessible Pinnacle)	985.8m	☐
164	256	Ben Vorlich	985.3m	☐
165	157	Druim Shionnach	985.2m	☐
166	158	Mullach na Dheiragain	982m	☐
167	159	An Gearanach	981.5m	☐
168	160	Stob Coire a' Chairn	981.3m	☐
169	161	Ciste Dhubh	981.1m	☐
170	162	Slioch	981m	☐
171	257	Meall nan Aighean	981m	☐
172	163	Maol Chinn-dearg	980.3m	☐
173	42	Beinn a' Chochuill	980m	☐
174	164	Stob Coire Sgriodain	979m	☐
175	276	Beinn Dubhchraig	978m	☐
176	165	Cona' Mheall	978m	☐
177	166	Stob Bàn	977m	☐
178	167	Meall nan Ceapraichean	977m	☐
179	258	Beinn a' Ghlò - Càrn Liath	976m	☐
180	24	Càrn a' Gheoidh	975m	☐
181	168	Beinn Sgritheall	974m	☐
182	277	Ben Lomond (Beinn Laomainn)	973.7m	☐
183	169	A' Mharconaich	973.2m	☐
184	268	Stuc a' Chroin	973m	☐
185	170	Sgurr a' Ghreadaidh	972.1m	☐
186	259	Meall Garbh	968m	☐
187	171	Aonach Eagach - Sgorr nam Fiannaidh	967.7m	☐
188	172	A' Mhaighdean	967m	☐
189	173	Sgùrr nan Gillean	966.1m	☐
190	43	Ben More	966m	☐
191	174	Sgurr na Banachdaich	965m	☐
192	260	Càrn a' Chlamain	963.5m	☐
193	175	Sgurr Thuilm	963m	☐
194	176	Ben Kilbreck - Meall nan Con	962.1m	☐
195	177	Sgorr Ruadh	960.7m	☐
196	261	Stuchd an Lochain	960m	☐

RANK	PAGE #	MUNRO	ALTITUDE	HIKED
197	44	Beinn nan Aighenan	960m	☐
198	278	Meall Glas	959.3m	☐
199	45	Beinn Fhionnlaidh	959m	☐
200	178	Bruach na Frithe	958.8m	☐
201	179	Buachaille Etive Beag - Stob Dubh	958m	☐
202	29	Tolmount	958m	☐
203	32	Tom Buidhe	957m	☐
204	180	Càrn Ghluasaid	957m	☐
205	181	Sgurr nan Coireachan	956m	☐
206	182	Saileag	956m	☐
207	233	Sgor Gaibhre	955m	☐
208	183	Beinn Liath Mhòr Fannaich	954m	☐
209	184	Sgurr nan Coireachan	953.8m	☐
210	185	Buachaille Etive Mòr - Stob na Bròige	953.4m	☐
211	262	Beinn Mhanach	953m	☐
212	186	Am Faochagach	953m	☐
213	187	Aonach Eagach - Meall Dearg	952.3m	☐
214	188	Meall Chuaich	951m	☐
215	189	Meall Gorm	949.7m	☐
216	46	Beinn Bhuidhe	948.5m	☐
217	190	Sgurr Mhic Choinnich	948.1m	☐
218	33	Driesh	947.6m	☐
219	191	Creag a' Mhaim	946.2m	☐
220	192	Meall Buidhe	946m	☐
221	193	Sgurr na Sgine	946m	☐
222	279	Beinn Tulaichean	945.8m	☐
223	194	Càrn Dearg	945.7m	☐
224	11	Càrn Bhac	945.1m	☐
225	55	Stob a' Choire Odhair	945m	☐
226	195	Bidein a' Choire Sheasgaich	945m	☐
227	12	An Socach	944m	☐
228	196	Sgurr Dubh Mor	944m	☐
229	47	Ben Vorlich	943m	☐
230	197	Binnein Beag	943m	☐
231	280	Beinn a' Chroin	941.4m	☐
232	234	Carn Dearg	941m	☐
233	235	Càrn na Caim	940.8m	☐
234	198	Mullach nan Coirean	939.3m	☐
235	30	Mount Keen (Monadh Caoin)	939m	☐
236	199	Luinne Bheinn	939m	☐
237	48	Beinn Sgulaird	937m	☐
238	200	Sron a' Choire Ghairbh	937m	☐
239	236	A' Bhuidheanach Bheag	936.1m	☐
240	201	Beinn na Lap	935m	☐
241	202	Meall a' Chrasgaidh	934m	☐
242	203	Am Basteir	934m	☐
243	204	Beinn Tarsuinn	933.8m	☐
244	205	Fionn Bheinn	933m	☐
245	206	Maoil Chean-dearg	933m	☐

RANK	PAGE #	MUNRO	ALTITUDE	HIKED
246	25	The Cairnwell	933M	☐
247	281	Beinn Chabhair	932.2M	☐
248	263	Meall Buidhe	932.1M	☐
249	264	Ben Chonzie	931M	☐
250	13	Beinn Bhreac	931M	☐
251	207	A' Chailleach	929.3M	☐
252	208	Blà Bheinn (Blaven)	929M	☐
253	34	Mayar	928.6M	☐
254	209	Moruisg	928M	☐
255	49	Meall nan Eun	928M	☐
256	210	Ben Hope (Beinn Hòb)	927M	☐
257	50	Beinn Narnain	927M	☐
258	211	Eididh nan Clach Geala	927M	☐
259	212	Sgurr nan Eag	926.3M	☐
260	213	Beinn Liath Mhòr	926M	☐
261	214	Seana Bhraigh	926M	☐
262	215	Geal Chàrn	926M	☐
263	265	Meall a' Choire Leith	925.6M	☐
264	216	Buachaille Etive Beag - Stob Coire Raineach	924.5M	☐
265	217	An Coileachan	924M	☐
266	218	Creag Pitridh	924M	☐
267	219	Sgurr nan Each	923M	☐
268	220	Beinn Alligin - Tom na Gruagaich	922M	☐
269	221	Carn Sgulain	920.3M	☐
270	282	Sgiath Chuil	920.1M	☐
271	222	An Socach	919.7M	☐
272	223	Gairich	919M	☐
273	224	Ruadh Stac Mor	918.7M	☐
274	225	A' Ghlas-bheinn	918M	☐
275	226	Sgurr a' Mhadaidh	918M	☐
276	227	Creag nan Damh	917.2M	☐
277	228	Geal-chàrn	917.1M	☐
278	229	Meall na Teanga	916.8M	☐
279	57	Beinn a' Chleibh	916.3M	☐
280	51	Ben Vane	915.76M	☐
281	14	Càrn Aosda	915.3M	☐
282	230	Beinn Teallach	914.6M	☐

COUNTY: ABERDEENSHIRE

CAIRN TOUL (CÀRN AN T-SABHAIL)

SECTION / REGION: 08A: CAIRNGORMS

| ALTITUDE: 1,291M | HEIGHT RANK: 4 | OS GRID REFERENCE: NN963972 |

DATE .... TOTAL TIME ....

START TIME .... END TIME ....

DISTANCE .... STEPS ....

STARTING POINT ....

COMPANION(S) ....

....

WEATHER

TEMPERATURE
....

WIND ....

NOTE .... DIFFICULTY ☆☆☆☆☆

....
....
....
....
....

1

COUNTY: ABERDEENSHIRE

SGOR AN LOCHAIN UAINE

SECTION / REGION: 08A: CAIRNGORMS

ALTITUDE: 1,258M   HEIGHT RANK: 5   OS GRID REFERENCE: NN956976

DATE .... TOTAL TIME ....
START TIME .... END TIME ....
DISTANCE .... STEPS ....
STARTING POINT ....
COMPANION(S) ....
....

WEATHER

TEMPERATURE
....
WIND ....

NOTE .... DIFFICULTY ☆☆☆☆☆

....
....
....
....
....

COUNTY: ABERDEENSHIRE

BEINN BHROTAIN

SECTION / REGION: 08A: CAIRNGORMS

ALTITUDE: 1,157M	HEIGHT RANK: 19	OS GRID REFERENCE: NN954922

DATE .... TOTAL TIME ....

START TIME .... END TIME ....

DISTANCE .... STEPS ....

STARTING POINT ....

COMPANION(S) ....

....

WEATHER

TEMPERATURE ....

WIND ....

NOTE .... DIFFICULTY ☆☆☆☆☆

....
....
....
....
....

COUNTY: ABERDEENSHIRE

LOCHNAGAR (BEINN CHÌOCHAN)

SECTION / REGION: 07A: BRAEMAR TO MONTROSE

ALTITUDE: 1,155.70M   HEIGHT RANK: 20   OS GRID REFERENCE: NO243861

DATE .... TOTAL TIME ....

START TIME .... END TIME ....

DISTANCE .... STEPS ....

STARTING POINT ....

COMPANION(S) ....

....

WEATHER

TEMPERATURE
....

WIND ....

NOTE .... DIFFICULTY ☆☆☆☆☆☆

....
....
....
....
....

COUNTY: ABERDEENSHIRE

DERRY CAIRNGORM (CÀRN GORM AN DOIRE)

SECTION / REGION: 08A: CAIRNGORMS

| ALTITUDE: 1,155M | HEIGHT RANK: 21 | OS GRID REFERENCE: NO017980 |

DATE .... TOTAL TIME ....

START TIME .... END TIME ....

DISTANCE .... STEPS ....

STARTING POINT ....

COMPANION(S) ....

....

WEATHER

TEMPERATURE
....

WIND ....

NOTE .... DIFFICULTY ☆☆☆☆☆

....
....
....
....
....

COUNTY: ABERDEENSHIRE

CÀRN A' CHOIRE BHOIDHEACH

SECTION / REGION: 07A: BRAEMAR TO MONTROSE

| ALTITUDE: 1,109.90M | HEIGHT RANK: 42 | OS GRID REFERENCE: NO226845 |

DATE .... TOTAL TIME ....

START TIME .... END TIME ....

DISTANCE .... STEPS ....

STARTING POINT ....

COMPANION(S) ....

....

WEATHER

TEMPERATURE ....

WIND ....

NOTE .... DIFFICULTY ☆☆☆☆☆

....
....
....
....
....

COUNTY: ABERDEENSHIRE

CÀRN AN T-SAGAIRT MÒR

SECTION / REGION: 07A: BRAEMAR TO MONTROSE

| ALTITUDE: 1,047M | HEIGHT RANK: 83 | OS GRID REFERENCE: NO208842 |

DATE .... TOTAL TIME ....

START TIME .... END TIME ....

DISTANCE .... STEPS ....

STARTING POINT ....

COMPANION(S) ....

....

WEATHER

TEMPERATURE
....
WIND ....

NOTE .... DIFFICULTY ☆☆☆☆☆

....
....
....
....
....

COUNTY: ABERDEENSHIRE

CÀRN A' MHAIM

SECTION / REGION: 08A: CAIRNGORMS

ALTITUDE: 1,037M   HEIGHT RANK: 95   OS GRID REFERENCE: NN994951

DATE .... TOTAL TIME ....

START TIME .... END TIME ....

DISTANCE .... STEPS ....

STARTING POINT ....

COMPANION(S) ....

....

WEATHER

TEMPERATURE ....

WIND ....

NOTE .... DIFFICULTY ☆☆☆☆☆

....
....
....
....
....

COUNTY: ABERDEENSHIRE

CÀRN AN TUIRC

SECTION / REGION: 07A: BRAEMAR TO MONTROSE

| ALTITUDE: 1,019M | HEIGHT RANK: 114 | OS GRID REFERENCE: NO174804 |

DATE .... TOTAL TIME ....

START TIME .... END TIME ....

DISTANCE .... STEPS ....

STARTING POINT ....

COMPANION(S) ....

....

WEATHER

TEMPERATURE
....
WIND ....

NOTE .... DIFFICULTY ☆☆☆☆☆

....
....
....
....
....

COUNTY: ABERDEENSHIRE

THE DEVIL'S POINT

SECTION / REGION: 08A: CAIRNGORMS

ALTITUDE: 1,006.90M   HEIGHT RANK: 125   OS GRID REFERENCE: NN976951

DATE .... TOTAL TIME ....

START TIME .... END TIME ....

DISTANCE .... STEPS ....

STARTING POINT ....

COMPANION(S) ....

....

WEATHER

TEMPERATURE
....
WIND ....

NOTE .... DIFFICULTY ☆☆☆☆☆

....
....
....
....
....

COUNTY: ABERDEENSHIRE

CÀRN BHAC

SECTION / REGION: 06B: PITLOCHRY TO BRAEMAR & BLAIRGOWRIE

ALTITUDE: 945.1M	HEIGHT RANK: 224	OS GRID REFERENCE: NO051832

DATE .... TOTAL TIME ....

START TIME .... END TIME ....

DISTANCE .... STEPS ....

STARTING POINT ....

COMPANION(S) ....

....

WEATHER

TEMPERATURE
....

WIND ....

NOTE .... DIFFICULTY ☆☆☆☆☆

....
....
....
....
....

COUNTY: ABERDEENSHIRE

AN SOCACH

SECTION / REGION: 06B: PITLOCHRY TO BRAEMAR & BLAIRGOWRIE

ALTITUDE: 944M HEIGHT RANK: 227 OS GRID REFERENCE: NO079800

DATE .... TOTAL TIME ....

START TIME .... END TIME ....

DISTANCE .... STEPS ....

STARTING POINT ....

COMPANION(S) ....

....

WEATHER

TEMPERATURE ....

WIND ....

NOTE .... DIFFICULTY ☆☆☆☆☆

....
....
....
....
....

COUNTY: ABERDEENSHIRE

BEINN BHREAC

SECTION / REGION: 08B: CAIRNGORMS

ALTITUDE: 931M	HEIGHT RANK: 250	OS GRID REFERENCE: NO058970

DATE .... TOTAL TIME ....

START TIME .... END TIME ....

DISTANCE .... STEPS ....

STARTING POINT ....

COMPANION(S) ....

....

WEATHER

TEMPERATURE ....

WIND ....

NOTE .... DIFFICULTY ☆☆☆☆☆

....
....
....
....
....

COUNTY: ABERDEENSHIRE

CÀRN AOSDA

SECTION / REGION: 06B: PITLOCHRY TO BRAEMAR & BLAIRGOWRIE

ALTITUDE: 915.3M   HEIGHT RANK: 281   OS GRID REFERENCE: NO133791

DATE .... TOTAL TIME ....

START TIME .... END TIME ....

DISTANCE .... STEPS ....

STARTING POINT ....

COMPANION(S) ....

....

WEATHER

TEMPERATURE
....

WIND ....

NOTE .... DIFFICULTY ☆☆☆☆☆

....
....
....
....
....

COUNTY: ABERDEENSHIRE / HIGHLAND

BRAERIACH (AM BRÀIGH RIABHACH)

SECTION / REGION: 08A: CAIRNGORMS

| ALTITUDE: 1,296M | HEIGHT RANK: 3 | OS GRID REFERENCE: NN953999 |

DATE .... TOTAL TIME ....

START TIME .... END TIME ....

DISTANCE .... STEPS ....

STARTING POINT ....

COMPANION(S) ....

....

WEATHER

TEMPERATURE ....

WIND ....

NOTE .... DIFFICULTY ☆☆☆☆☆

....
....
....
....
....

COUNTY: ABERDEENSHIRE / HIGHLAND

MONADH MÒR

SECTION / REGION: 08A: CAIRNGORMS

ALTITUDE: 1,113M   HEIGHT RANK: 40   OS GRID REFERENCE: NN938942

DATE .... TOTAL TIME ....

START TIME .... END TIME ....

DISTANCE .... STEPS ....

STARTING POINT ....

COMPANION(S) ....

....

WEATHER

TEMPERATURE ....

WIND ....

NOTE .... DIFFICULTY ☆☆☆☆☆

....
....
....
....
....

NTY: ABERDEENSHIRE/ HIGHLAND/ PERTH AND KINR

CARN AN FHIDHLEIR

SECTION / REGION: 06A: GLEN TROMIE TO GLEN TILT

| ALTITUDE: 994M | HEIGHT RANK: 149 | OS GRID REFERENCE: NN904841 |

DATE .... TOTAL TIME ....

START TIME .... END TIME ....

DISTANCE .... STEPS ....

STARTING POINT ....

COMPANION(S) ....

....

WEATHER

TEMPERATURE
....
WIND ....

NOTE .... DIFFICULTY ☆☆☆☆☆

....
....
....
....
....

COUNTY: ABERDEENSHIRE / MORAY

BEN MACDUI (BEINN MACDUIBH)

SECTION / REGION: 08A: CAIRNGORMS

ALTITUDE: 1,309M   HEIGHT RANK: 2   OS GRID REFERENCE: NN988989

DATE .... TOTAL TIME ....

START TIME .... END TIME ....

DISTANCE .... STEPS ....

STARTING POINT ....

COMPANION(S) ....

....

WEATHER

TEMPERATURE
....

WIND ....

NOTE .... DIFFICULTY ☆☆☆☆☆

....

....

....

....

....

COUNTY: ABERDEENSHIRE/ MORAY

BEINN A' BHÙIRD

SECTION / REGION: 08B: CAIRNGORMS

| ALTITUDE: 1,197M | HEIGHT RANK: 11 | OS GRID REFERENCE: NJ092006 |

DATE .... TOTAL TIME ....

START TIME .... END TIME ....

DISTANCE .... STEPS ....

STARTING POINT ....

COMPANION(S) ....

....

WEATHER

TEMPERATURE
....

WIND ....

NOTE .... DIFFICULTY ☆☆☆☆☆

....
....
....
....
....

COUNTY: ABERDEENSHIRE / MORAY

BEN AVON (BEINN ATHFHINN)

SECTION / REGION: 08B: CAIRNGORMS

| ALTITUDE: 1,172M | HEIGHT RANK: 17 | OS GRID REFERENCE: NJ131018 |

DATE .... TOTAL TIME ....

START TIME .... END TIME ....

DISTANCE .... STEPS ....

STARTING POINT ....

COMPANION(S) ....

....

WEATHER

TEMPERATURE ....

WIND ....

NOTE .... DIFFICULTY ☆☆☆☆☆

....
....
....
....
....

COUNTY: ABERDEENSHIRE/ MORAY

BEINN A' CHAORAINN

SECTION / REGION: 08B: CAIRNGORMS

ALTITUDE: 1,083M   HEIGHT RANK: 60   OS GRID REFERENCE: NJ045013

DATE .... TOTAL TIME ....

START TIME .... END TIME ....

DISTANCE .... STEPS ....

STARTING POINT ....

COMPANION(S) ....

....

WEATHER

TEMPERATURE
....
WIND ....

NOTE .... DIFFICULTY ☆☆☆☆☆

....
....
....
....
....

COUNTY: ABERDEENSHIRE / PERTH AND KINROSS

BEINN IUTHARN MHÒR

SECTION / REGION: 06B: PITLOCHRY TO BRAEMAR & BLAIRGOWRIE

ALTITUDE: 1,045M   HEIGHT RANK: 88   OS GRID REFERENCE: NO045792

DATE .... TOTAL TIME ....

START TIME .... END TIME ....

DISTANCE .... STEPS ....

STARTING POINT ....

COMPANION(S) ....

....

WEATHER

TEMPERATURE ....

WIND ....

NOTE .... DIFFICULTY ☆☆☆☆☆

....
....
....
....
....

COUNTY: ABERDEENSHIRE / PERTH AND KINROSS

AN SGARSOCH

SECTION / REGION: 06A: GLEN TROMIE TO GLEN TILT

ALTITUDE: 1,006.50M   HEIGHT RANK: 126   OS GRID REFERENCE: NN933836

DATE .... TOTAL TIME ....

START TIME .... END TIME ....

DISTANCE .... STEPS ....

STARTING POINT ....

COMPANION(S) ....

....

WEATHER

TEMPERATURE
....

WIND ....

NOTE .... DIFFICULTY ☆☆☆☆☆

....

....

....

....

....

COUNTY: ABERDEENSHIRE / PERTH AND KINROSS

CÀRN A' GHEOIDH

SECTION / REGION: 06B: PITLOCHRY TO BRAEMAR & BLAIRGOWRIE

ALTITUDE: 975M   HEIGHT RANK: 180   OS GRID REFERENCE: NO107767

DATE .... TOTAL TIME ....

START TIME .... END TIME ....

DISTANCE .... STEPS ....

STARTING POINT ....

COMPANION(S) ....

....

WEATHER   TEMPERATURE
                                     ....
                                     WIND ....

NOTE .... DIFFICULTY ☆☆☆☆☆

....
....
....
....
....

COUNTY: ABERDEENSHIRE / PERTH AND KINROSS

THE CAIRNWELL

SECTION / REGION: 06B: PITLOCHRY TO BRAEMAR & BLAIRGOWRIE

| ALTITUDE: 933M | HEIGHT RANK: 246 | OS GRID REFERENCE: NO134773 |

DATE .... TOTAL TIME ....

START TIME .... END TIME ....

DISTANCE .... STEPS ....

STARTING POINT ....

COMPANION(S) ....

....

WEATHER

TEMPERATURE ....

WIND ....

NOTE .... DIFFICULTY ☆☆☆☆☆

....
....
....
....
....

COUNTY: ABERDEENSHIRE/ANGUS

CAIRN OF CLAISE

SECTION / REGION: 07A: BRAEMAR TO MONTROSE

ALTITUDE: 1,064M   HEIGHT RANK: 71   OS GRID REFERENCE: NO185788

DATE .... TOTAL TIME ....

START TIME .... END TIME ....

DISTANCE .... STEPS ....

STARTING POINT ....

COMPANION(S) ....

....

WEATHER

TEMPERATURE ....

WIND ....

NOTE .... DIFFICULTY ☆☆☆☆☆

....
....
....
....
....

COUNTY: ABERDEENSHIRE/ANGUS

CAIRN BANNOCH

SECTION / REGION: 07A: BRAEMAR TO MONTROSE

| ALTITUDE: 1,012M | HEIGHT RANK: 118 | OS GRID REFERENCE: NO222825 |

DATE .... TOTAL TIME ....

START TIME .... END TIME ....

DISTANCE .... STEPS ....

STARTING POINT ....

COMPANION(S) ....

....

WEATHER

TEMPERATURE ....

WIND ....

NOTE .... DIFFICULTY ☆☆☆☆☆

....
....
....
....
....

COUNTY: ABERDEENSHIRE/ANGUS

BROAD CAIRN

SECTION / REGION: 07A: BRAEMAR TO MONTROSE

| ALTITUDE: 998M | HEIGHT RANK: 144 | OS GRID REFERENCE: NO240815 |

DATE .... TOTAL TIME ....

START TIME .... END TIME ....

DISTANCE .... STEPS ....

STARTING POINT ....

COMPANION(S) ....

....

WEATHER

TEMPERATURE ....

WIND ....

NOTE .... DIFFICULTY ☆☆☆☆☆

....
....
....
....
....

COUNTY: ABERDEENSHIRE/ANGUS

TOLMOUNT

SECTION / REGION: 07A: BRAEMAR TO MONTROSE

ALTITUDE: 958M　　HEIGHT RANK: 202　　OS GRID REFERENCE: NO210800

DATE .... TOTAL TIME ....

START TIME .... END TIME ....

DISTANCE .... STEPS ....

STARTING POINT ....

COMPANION(S) ....

....

WEATHER

TEMPERATURE ....

WIND ....

NOTE .... DIFFICULTY ☆☆☆☆☆

....
....
....
....
....

COUNTY: ABERDEENSHIRE/ANGUS

MOUNT KEEN (MONADH CAOIN)

SECTION / REGION: 07B: BRAEMAR TO MONTROSE

| ALTITUDE: 939M | HEIGHT RANK: 235 | OS GRID REFERENCE: NO409869 |

DATE .... TOTAL TIME ....

START TIME .... END TIME ....

DISTANCE .... STEPS ....

STARTING POINT ....

COMPANION(S) ....

....

WEATHER

TEMPERATURE ....

WIND ....

NOTE .... DIFFICULTY ☆☆☆☆☆

....
....
....
....
....

COUNTY: ANGUS

GLAS MAOL

SECTION / REGION: 07A: BRAEMAR TO MONTROSE

ALTITUDE: 1,068M HEIGHT RANK: 70 OS GRID REFERENCE: NO166765

DATE .... TOTAL TIME ....

START TIME .... END TIME ....

DISTANCE .... STEPS ....

STARTING POINT ....

COMPANION(S) ....

....

WEATHER

TEMPERATURE
....
WIND ....

NOTE .... DIFFICULTY ☆☆☆☆☆

....
....
....
....
....

COUNTY: ANGUS

TOM BUIDHE

SECTION / REGION: 07A: BRAEMAR TO MONTROSE

ALTITUDE: 957M   HEIGHT RANK: 203   OS GRID REFERENCE: NO213787

DATE .... TOTAL TIME ....

START TIME .... END TIME ....

DISTANCE .... STEPS ....

STARTING POINT ....

COMPANION(S) ....

....

WEATHER

TEMPERATURE
....
WIND ....

NOTE .... DIFFICULTY ☆☆☆☆☆

....
....
....
....
....

COUNTY: ANGUS

DRIESH

SECTION / REGION: 07A: BRAEMAR TO MONTROSE

ALTITUDE: 947.6M   HEIGHT RANK: 218   OS GRID REFERENCE: NO271735

DATE .... TOTAL TIME ....

START TIME .... END TIME ....

DISTANCE .... STEPS ....

STARTING POINT ....

COMPANION(S) ....

....

WEATHER

TEMPERATURE
....
WIND ....

NOTE .... DIFFICULTY ☆☆☆☆☆

....
....
....
....
....

COUNTY: ANGUS

MAYAR

SECTION / REGION: 07A: BRAEMAR TO MONTROSE

ALTITUDE: 928.6M   HEIGHT RANK: 253   OS GRID REFERENCE: NO240737

DATE .... TOTAL TIME ....

START TIME .... END TIME ....

DISTANCE .... STEPS ....

STARTING POINT ....

COMPANION(S) ....

....

WEATHER

TEMPERATURE
....

WIND ....

NOTE .... DIFFICULTY ☆☆☆☆☆

....
....
....
....
....

COUNTY: ANGUS/ PERTH AND KINROSS

CREAG LEACACH

SECTION / REGION: 07A: BRAEMAR TO MONTROSE

| ALTITUDE: 988.2M | HEIGHT RANK: 158 | OS GRID REFERENCE: NO154745 |

DATE .... TOTAL TIME ....

START TIME .... END TIME ....

DISTANCE .... STEPS ....

STARTING POINT ....

COMPANION(S) ....

....

WEATHER

TEMPERATURE ....

WIND ....

NOTE .... DIFFICULTY ☆☆☆☆☆

....
....
....
....
....

COUNTY: ARGYLL AND BUTE

BEN CRUACHAN

SECTION / REGION: 03C: GLEN ETIVE TO GLEN LOCHY

ALTITUDE: 1,127M HEIGHT RANK: 31 OS GRID REFERENCE: NN069304

DATE .... TOTAL TIME ....

START TIME .... END TIME ....

DISTANCE .... STEPS ....

STARTING POINT ....

COMPANION(S) ....

....

WEATHER

TEMPERATURE
....
WIND ....

NOTE .... DIFFICULTY ☆☆☆☆☆

....
....
....
....
....

COUNTY: ARGYLL AND BUTE

BEINN DORAIN

SECTION / REGION: 02A: LOCH RANNOCH TO GLEN LYON

| ALTITUDE: 1,076M | HEIGHT RANK: 64 | OS GRID REFERENCE: NN325378 |

DATE .... TOTAL TIME ....

START TIME .... END TIME ....

DISTANCE .... STEPS ....

STARTING POINT ....

COMPANION(S) ....

....

WEATHER

TEMPERATURE
....
WIND ....

NOTE .... DIFFICULTY ☆☆☆☆☆

....
....
....
....
....

COUNTY: ARGYLL AND BUTE

BEINN ÌME

SECTION / REGION: 01D: INVERARAY TO CRIANLARICH

ALTITUDE: 1,012.20M   HEIGHT RANK: 117   OS GRID REFERENCE: NN254084

DATE .... TOTAL TIME ....

START TIME .... END TIME ....

DISTANCE .... STEPS ....

STARTING POINT ....

COMPANION(S) ....

....

WEATHER

TEMPERATURE ....

WIND ....

NOTE .... DIFFICULTY ☆☆☆☆☆

....
....
....
....
....

COUNTY: ARGYLL AND BUTE

BEINN AN DOTHAIDH

SECTION / REGION: 02A: LOCH RANNOCH TO GLEN LYON

| ALTITUDE: 1,004M | HEIGHT RANK: 130 | OS GRID REFERENCE: NN331408 |

DATE .... TOTAL TIME ....

START TIME .... END TIME ....

DISTANCE .... STEPS ....

STARTING POINT ....

COMPANION(S) ....

....

WEATHER

TEMPERATURE ....

WIND ....

NOTE .... DIFFICULTY ☆☆☆☆☆

....
....
....
....
....

COUNTY: ARGYLL AND BUTE

STOB DAIMH

SECTION / REGION: 03C: GLEN ETIVE TO GLEN LOCHY

ALTITUDE: 999.2M   HEIGHT RANK: 140   OS GRID REFERENCE: NN094308

DATE .... TOTAL TIME ....

START TIME .... END TIME ....

DISTANCE .... STEPS ....

STARTING POINT ....

COMPANION(S) ....

....

WEATHER

TEMPERATURE ....

WIND ....

NOTE .... DIFFICULTY ☆☆☆☆☆

....
....
....
....
....

COUNTY: ARGYLL AND BUTE

BEINN EUNAICH

SECTION / REGION: 03C: GLEN ETIVE TO GLEN LOCHY

ALTITUDE: 989M **HEIGHT RANK: 156** **OS GRID REFERENCE: NN135327**

DATE .... TOTAL TIME ....

START TIME .... END TIME ....

DISTANCE .... STEPS ....

STARTING POINT ....

COMPANION(S) ....

....

WEATHER

TEMPERATURE ....

WIND ....

NOTE .... DIFFICULTY ☆☆☆☆☆

....
....
....
....
....

COUNTY: ARGYLL AND BUTE

BEINN A' CHOCHUILL

SECTION / REGION: 03C: GLEN ETIVE TO GLEN LOCHY

ALTITUDE: 980M   HEIGHT RANK: 173   OS GRID REFERENCE: NN109328

DATE .... TOTAL TIME ....

START TIME .... END TIME ....

DISTANCE .... STEPS ....

STARTING POINT ....

COMPANION(S) ....

....

WEATHER

TEMPERATURE
....
WIND ....

NOTE .... DIFFICULTY ☆☆☆☆☆

....
....
....
....
....

COUNTY: ARGYLL AND BUTE

BEN MORE

SECTION / REGION: 17E: MULL AND NEARBY ISLANDS

| ALTITUDE: 966M | HEIGHT RANK: 190 | OS GRID REFERENCE: NM525330 |

DATE .... TOTAL TIME ....

START TIME .... END TIME ....

DISTANCE .... STEPS ....

STARTING POINT ....

COMPANION(S) ....

....

WEATHER

TEMPERATURE
....

WIND ....

NOTE .... DIFFICULTY ☆☆☆☆☆

....
....
....
....
....

COUNTY: ARGYLL AND BUTE

BEINN NAN AIGHENAN

SECTION / REGION: 03C: GLEN ETIVE TO GLEN LOCHY

ALTITUDE: 960M   HEIGHT RANK: 197   OS GRID REFERENCE: NN148405

DATE .... TOTAL TIME ....

START TIME .... END TIME ....

DISTANCE .... STEPS ....

STARTING POINT ....

COMPANION(S) ....

....

WEATHER

TEMPERATURE
....
WIND ....

NOTE .... DIFFICULTY ☆☆☆☆☆

....
....
....
....
....

COUNTY: ARGYLL AND BUTE

BEINN FHIONNLAIDH

SECTION / REGION: 03B: LOCH LINNHE TO LOCH ETIVE

| ALTITUDE: 959M | HEIGHT RANK: 199 | OS GRID REFERENCE: NN095497 |

DATE .... TOTAL TIME ....

START TIME .... END TIME ....

DISTANCE .... STEPS ....

STARTING POINT ....

COMPANION(S) ....

....

WEATHER

TEMPERATURE ....

WIND ....

NOTE .... DIFFICULTY ☆☆☆☆☆

....
....
....
....
....

COUNTY: ARGYLL AND BUTE

BEINN BHUIDHE

SECTION / REGION: 01D: INVERARAY TO CRIANLARICH

ALTITUDE: 948.5M HEIGHT RANK: 216 OS GRID REFERENCE: NN203187

DATE .... TOTAL TIME ....

START TIME .... END TIME ....

DISTANCE .... STEPS ....

STARTING POINT ....

COMPANION(S) ....

....

WEATHER

TEMPERATURE ....

WIND ....

NOTE .... DIFFICULTY ☆☆☆☆☆

....
....
....
....
....

COUNTY: ARGYLL AND BUTE

BEN VORLICH

SECTION / REGION: OLD: INVERARAY TO CRIANLARICH

| ALTITUDE: 943M | HEIGHT RANK: 229 | OS GRID REFERENCE: NN295124 |

DATE .... TOTAL TIME ....

START TIME .... END TIME ....

DISTANCE .... STEPS ....

STARTING POINT ....

COMPANION(S) ....

....

WEATHER

TEMPERATURE ....

WIND ....

NOTE .... DIFFICULTY ☆☆☆☆☆

....

....

....

....

....

COUNTY: ARGYLL AND BUTE

BEINN SGULAIRD

SECTION / REGION: 03B: LOCH LINNHE TO LOCH ETIVE

ALTITUDE: 937M   HEIGHT RANK: 237   OS GRID REFERENCE: NN053460

DATE .... TOTAL TIME ....

START TIME .... END TIME ....

DISTANCE .... STEPS ....

STARTING POINT ....

COMPANION(S) ....

....

WEATHER

TEMPERATURE ....

WIND ....

NOTE .... DIFFICULTY ☆☆☆☆☆

....
....
....
....
....

COUNTY: ARGYLL AND BUTE

MEALL NAN EUN

SECTION / REGION: 03C: GLEN ETIVE TO GLEN LOCHY

| ALTITUDE: 928M | HEIGHT RANK: 255 | OS GRID REFERENCE: NN192449 |

DATE .... TOTAL TIME ....

START TIME .... END TIME ....

DISTANCE .... STEPS ....

STARTING POINT ....

COMPANION(S) ....

....

WEATHER

TEMPERATURE ....

WIND ....

NOTE .... DIFFICULTY ☆☆☆☆☆

....
....
....
....
....

COUNTY: ARGYLL AND BUTE

BEINN NARNAIN

SECTION / REGION: 01D: INVERARAY TO CRIANLARICH

| ALTITUDE: 927M | HEIGHT RANK: 257 | OS GRID REFERENCE: NN271066 |

DATE .... TOTAL TIME ....

START TIME .... END TIME ....

DISTANCE .... STEPS ....

STARTING POINT ....

COMPANION(S) ....

....

WEATHER

TEMPERATURE ....

WIND ....

NOTE .... DIFFICULTY ☆☆☆☆☆

....
....
....
....
....

COUNTY: ARGYLL AND BUTE

BEN VANE

SECTION / REGION: 01D: INVERARAY TO CRIANLARICH

ALTITUDE: 915.76M   HEIGHT RANK: 280   OS GRID REFERENCE: NN277098

DATE .... TOTAL TIME ....

START TIME .... END TIME ....

DISTANCE .... STEPS ....

STARTING POINT ....

COMPANION(S) ....

....

WEATHER

TEMPERATURE ....

WIND ....

NOTE .... DIFFICULTY ☆☆☆☆☆

....
....
....
....
....

COUNTY: ARGYLL AND BUTE / HIGHLAND

STOB GHABHAR

SECTION / REGION: 03C: GLEN ETIVE TO GLEN LOCHY

ALTITUDE: 1,090M   HEIGHT RANK: 54   OS GRID REFERENCE: NN230455

DATE .... TOTAL TIME ....

START TIME .... END TIME ....

DISTANCE .... STEPS ....

STARTING POINT ....

COMPANION(S) ....

....

WEATHER

TEMPERATURE ....

WIND ....

NOTE .... DIFFICULTY ☆☆☆☆☆

....
....
....
....
....

COUNTY: ARGYLL AND BUTE / HIGHLAND

STOB COIR'AN ALBANNAICH

SECTION / REGION: 03C: GLEN ETIVE TO GLEN LOCHY

ALTITUDE: 1,044M HEIGHT RANK: 89 OS GRID REFERENCE: NN169443

DATE .... TOTAL TIME ....

START TIME .... END TIME ....

DISTANCE .... STEPS ....

STARTING POINT ....

COMPANION(S) ....

....

WEATHER

TEMPERATURE ....

WIND ....

NOTE .... DIFFICULTY ☆☆☆☆☆

....
....
....
....
....

COUNTY: ARGYLL AND BUTE / HIGHLAND

GLAS BHEINN MHÒR

SECTION / REGION: 03C: GLEN ETIVE TO GLEN LOCHY

| ALTITUDE: 997.7M | HEIGHT RANK: 145 | OS GRID REFERENCE: NN153429 |

DATE .... TOTAL TIME ....

START TIME .... END TIME ....

DISTANCE .... STEPS ....

STARTING POINT ....

COMPANION(S) ....

....

WEATHER

TEMPERATURE ....

WIND ....

NOTE .... DIFFICULTY ☆☆☆☆☆

....
....
....
....
....

COUNTY: ARGYLL AND BUTE / HIGHLAND

STOB A' CHOIRE ODHAIR

SECTION / REGION: 03C: GLEN ETIVE TO GLEN LOCHY

| ALTITUDE: 945M | HEIGHT RANK: 225 | OS GRID REFERENCE: NN257459 |

DATE .... TOTAL TIME ....

START TIME .... END TIME ....

DISTANCE .... STEPS ....

STARTING POINT ....

COMPANION(S) ....

....

WEATHER

TEMPERATURE ....

WIND ....

NOTE .... DIFFICULTY ☆☆☆☆☆

....
....
....
....
....

COUNTY: ARGYLL AND BUTE / PERTH AND KINROSS

BEINN ACHALADAIR

SECTION / REGION: 02A: LOCH RANNOCH TO GLEN LYON

ALTITUDE: 1,038.60M HEIGHT RANK: 94 OS GRID REFERENCE: NN344432

DATE .... TOTAL TIME ....

START TIME .... END TIME ....

DISTANCE .... STEPS ....

STARTING POINT ....

COMPANION(S) ....

....

WEATHER

TEMPERATURE
....

WIND ....

NOTE .... DIFFICULTY ☆☆☆☆☆

....
....
....
....
....

COUNTY: ARGYLL AND BUTE / STIRLING

BEINN A' CHLEIBH

SECTION / REGION: 01D: INVERARAY TO CRIANLARICH

ALTITUDE: 916.3M   HEIGHT RANK: 279   OS GRID REFERENCE: NN250256

DATE .... TOTAL TIME ....

START TIME .... END TIME ....

DISTANCE .... STEPS ....

STARTING POINT ....

COMPANION(S) ....

....

WEATHER

TEMPERATURE ....

WIND ....

NOTE .... DIFFICULTY ☆☆☆☆☆

....
....
....
....
....

COUNTY: HIGHLAND

BEN NEVIS (BEINN NIBHEIS)

SECTION / REGION: 04A: FORT WILLIAM TO LOCH TREIG & LOCH LEVEN

ALTITUDE: 1,344.53M   HEIGHT RANK: 1   OS GRID REFERENCE: NN166712

DATE .... TOTAL TIME ....

START TIME .... END TIME ....

DISTANCE .... STEPS ....

STARTING POINT ....

COMPANION(S) ....

....

WEATHER   TEMPERATURE
☀ ⛅ 🌤 🌧 ⛈ ❄   ....
● ● ● ● ● ●   WIND ....

NOTE .... DIFFICULTY ☆☆☆☆☆

....

....

....

....

....

COUNTY: HIGHLAND

AONACH BEAG

SECTION / REGION: 04A: FORT WILLIAM TO LOCH TREIG & LOCH LEVEN

| ALTITUDE: 1,234M | HEIGHT RANK: 7 | OS GRID REFERENCE: NN197715 |

DATE .... TOTAL TIME ....

START TIME .... END TIME ....

DISTANCE .... STEPS ....

STARTING POINT ....

COMPANION(S) ....

....

WEATHER

TEMPERATURE ....

WIND ....

NOTE .... DIFFICULTY ☆☆☆☆☆

....
....
....
....
....

COUNTY: HIGHLAND

AONACH MÒR

SECTION / REGION: 04A: FORT WILLIAM TO LOCH TREIG & LOCH LEVEN

ALTITUDE: 1,220.40M　　HEIGHT RANK: 8　　OS GRID REFERENCE: NN193729

DATE .... TOTAL TIME ....

START TIME .... END TIME ....

DISTANCE .... STEPS ....

STARTING POINT ....

COMPANION(S) ....

....

WEATHER

TEMPERATURE ....

WIND ....

NOTE .... DIFFICULTY ☆☆☆☆☆

....

....

....

....

....

COUNTY: HIGHLAND

CÀRN MÒR DEARG

SECTION / REGION: 04A: FORT WILLIAM TO LOCH TREIG & LOCH LEVEN

ALTITUDE: 1,220M   HEIGHT RANK: 9   OS GRID REFERENCE: NN177721

DATE .... TOTAL TIME ....

START TIME................................. END TIME ....

DISTANCE.................................... STEPS ....

STARTING POINT ....

COMPANION(S) ....

....

WEATHER

TEMPERATURE ....

WIND ....

NOTE .... DIFFICULTY ☆☆☆☆☆

COUNTY: HIGHLAND

CÀRN EIGE

SECTION / REGION: 11A: LOCH DUICH TO CANNICH

ALTITUDE: 1,182.80M   HEIGHT RANK: 13   OS GRID REFERENCE: NH123261

DATE .... TOTAL TIME ....

START TIME .... END TIME ....

DISTANCE .... STEPS ....

STARTING POINT ....

COMPANION(S) ....

....

WEATHER

TEMPERATURE ....

WIND ....

NOTE .... DIFFICULTY ☆☆☆☆☆

....
....
....
....
....

COUNTY: HIGHLAND

MAM SODHAIL

SECTION / REGION: 11A: LOCH DUICH TO CANNICH

ALTITUDE: 1,179.40M   HEIGHT RANK: 14   OS GRID REFERENCE: NH120253

DATE .... TOTAL TIME ....

START TIME .... END TIME ....

DISTANCE .... STEPS ....

STARTING POINT ....

COMPANION(S) ....

....

WEATHER   TEMPERATURE
                                         ....
                                         WIND ....

NOTE .... DIFFICULTY ☆☆☆☆☆

....
....
....
....
....

COUNTY: HIGHLAND

STOB CHOIRE CLAURIGH

SECTION / REGION: 04A: FORT WILLIAM TO LOCH TREIG & LOCH LEVEN

ALTITUDE: 1,177M   HEIGHT RANK: 15   OS GRID REFERENCE: NN261738

DATE .... TOTAL TIME ....

START TIME .... END TIME ....

DISTANCE .... STEPS ....

STARTING POINT ....

COMPANION(S) ....

....

WEATHER

TEMPERATURE ....

WIND ....

NOTE .... DIFFICULTY ☆☆☆☆☆

....
....
....
....
....

COUNTY: HIGHLAND

SGURR NAN CEATHREAMHNAN

SECTION / REGION: 11A: LOCH DUICH TO CANNICH

ALTITUDE: 1,151M   HEIGHT RANK: 22   OS GRID REFERENCE: NH057228

DATE .... TOTAL TIME ....

START TIME .... END TIME ....

DISTANCE .... STEPS ....

STARTING POINT ....

COMPANION(S) ....

....

WEATHER   TEMPERATURE

WIND ....

NOTE .... DIFFICULTY ☆☆☆☆☆

....

....

....

....

....

COUNTY: HIGHLAND

SGURR NA LAPAICH

SECTION / REGION: 12B: KILLILAN TO INVERNESS

ALTITUDE: 1,151M HEIGHT RANK: 23 OS GRID REFERENCE: NH161351

DATE .... TOTAL TIME ....

START TIME .... END TIME ....

DISTANCE .... STEPS ....

STARTING POINT ....

COMPANION(S) ....

....

WEATHER

TEMPERATURE ....

WIND ....

NOTE .... DIFFICULTY ☆☆☆☆☆

....
....
....
....
....

COUNTY: HIGHLAND

BIDEAN NAM BIAN

SECTION / REGION: 03B: LOCH LINNHE TO LOCH ETIVE

| ALTITUDE: 1,149.40M | HEIGHT RANK: 24 | OS GRID REFERENCE: NN143542 |

DATE .... TOTAL TIME ....

START TIME .... END TIME ....

DISTANCE .... STEPS ....

STARTING POINT ....

COMPANION(S) ....

....

WEATHER

TEMPERATURE
....
WIND ....

NOTE .... DIFFICULTY ☆☆☆☆☆

....
....
....
....
....

COUNTY: HIGHLAND

BEN ALDER (BEINN EALLAIR)

SECTION / REGION: 04B: LOCH TREIG TO LOCH ERICHT

ALTITUDE: 1,148M   HEIGHT RANK: 25   OS GRID REFERENCE: NN496718

DATE .... TOTAL TIME ....

START TIME .... END TIME ....

DISTANCE .... STEPS ....

STARTING POINT ....

COMPANION(S) ....

....

WEATHER

☀ ☁ ⛅ 🌧 ⛈ ❄
● ● ● ● ● ●

TEMPERATURE
....

WIND ....

NOTE .... DIFFICULTY ☆☆☆☆☆

....

....

....

....

....

COUNTY: HIGHLAND

GEAL-CHÀRN

SECTION / REGION: 04B: LOCH TREIG TO LOCH ERICHT

ALTITUDE: 1,132M   **HEIGHT RANK: 26**   **OS GRID REFERENCE: NN469746**

DATE .... TOTAL TIME ....

START TIME .... END TIME ....

DISTANCE .... STEPS ....

STARTING POINT ....

COMPANION(S) ....

....

WEATHER   TEMPERATURE ....

WIND ....

NOTE .... DIFFICULTY ☆☆☆☆☆

....
....
....
....
....

COUNTY: HIGHLAND

BINNEIN MÒR

SECTION / REGION: 04A: FORT WILLIAM TO LOCH TREIG & LOCH LEVEN

ALTITUDE: 1,130M   HEIGHT RANK: 28   OS GRID REFERENCE: NN212663

DATE .... TOTAL TIME ....

START TIME .... END TIME ....

DISTANCE .... STEPS ....

STARTING POINT ....

COMPANION(S) ....

....

WEATHER

TEMPERATURE ....

WIND ....

NOTE .... DIFFICULTY ☆☆☆☆☆

....
....
....
....
....

COUNTY: HIGHLAND

AN RIABHACHAN

SECTION / REGION: 12B: KILLILAN TO INVERNESS

ALTITUDE: 1,129M   HEIGHT RANK: 29   OS GRID REFERENCE: NH133344

DATE .... TOTAL TIME ....

START TIME .... END TIME ....

DISTANCE .... STEPS ....

STARTING POINT ....

COMPANION(S) ....

....

WEATHER

TEMPERATURE ....

WIND ....

NOTE .... DIFFICULTY ☆☆☆☆☆

....
....
....
....
....

COUNTY: HIGHLAND

CREAG MEAGAIDH

SECTION / REGION: 09C: LOCH LOCHY TO LOCH LAGGAN

ALTITUDE: 1,128.10M   HEIGHT RANK: 30   OS GRID REFERENCE: NN418875

DATE .... TOTAL TIME ....

START TIME .... END TIME ....

DISTANCE .... STEPS ....

STARTING POINT ....

COMPANION(S) ....

....

WEATHER

TEMPERATURE ....

WIND ....

NOTE .... DIFFICULTY ☆☆☆☆☆

....
....
....
....
....

COUNTY: HIGHLAND

A' CHRAILEAG (A' CHRÀLAIG)

SECTION / REGION: 11B: GLEN AFFRIC TO GLEN MORISTON

ALTITUDE: 1,120M   HEIGHT RANK: 34   OS GRID REFERENCE: NH094147

DATE .... TOTAL TIME ....

START TIME .... END TIME ....

DISTANCE .... STEPS ....

STARTING POINT ....

COMPANION(S) ....

....

WEATHER

TEMPERATURE
....
WIND ....

NOTE .... DIFFICULTY ☆☆☆☆☆

....
....
....
....
....

COUNTY: HIGHLAND

SGOR GAOITH

SECTION / REGION: 08A: CAIRNGORMS

| ALTITUDE: 1,118M | HEIGHT RANK: 35 | OS GRID REFERENCE: NN903989 |

DATE .... TOTAL TIME ....

START TIME .... END TIME ....

DISTANCE .... STEPS ....

STARTING POINT ....

COMPANION(S) ....

....

WEATHER

TEMPERATURE ....

WIND ....

NOTE .... DIFFICULTY ☆☆☆☆☆

....
....
....
....
....

COUNTY: HIGHLAND

STOB COIRE AN LAOIGH

SECTION / REGION: 04A: FORT WILLIAM TO LOCH TREIG & LOCH LEVEN

ALTITUDE: 1,116M **HEIGHT RANK: 37** **OS GRID REFERENCE: NN239725**

DATE .... TOTAL TIME ....

START TIME .... END TIME ....

DISTANCE .... STEPS ....

STARTING POINT ....

COMPANION(S) ....

....

WEATHER　　　　　　　　　　　TEMPERATURE

　　　　　　　　　　　　　　　　　WIND ....

NOTE .... DIFFICULTY ☆☆☆☆☆

....

....

....

....

....

COUNTY: HIGHLAND

AONACH BEAG

SECTION / REGION: 04B: LOCH TREIG TO LOCH ERICHT

ALTITUDE: 1,115.80M   HEIGHT RANK: 38   OS GRID REFERENCE: NN457741

DATE .... TOTAL TIME ....

START TIME .... END TIME ....

DISTANCE .... STEPS ....

STARTING POINT ....

COMPANION(S) ....

....

WEATHER

TEMPERATURE ....

WIND ....

NOTE .... DIFFICULTY ☆☆☆☆☆

....
....
....
....
....

COUNTY: HIGHLAND

STOB COIRE EASAIN

SECTION / REGION: 04A: FORT WILLIAM TO LOCH TREIG & LOCH LEVEN

| ALTITUDE: 1,115M | HEIGHT RANK: 39 | OS GRID REFERENCE: NN308730 |

DATE .... TOTAL TIME ....

START TIME.................................... END TIME ....

DISTANCE...................................... STEPS ....

STARTING POINT ....

COMPANION(S) ....

....

WEATHER

TEMPERATURE ....

WIND ....

NOTE .... DIFFICULTY ☆☆☆☆☆

COUNTY: HIGHLAND

TOM A' CHOINICH

SECTION / REGION: 11A: LOCH DUICH TO CANNICH

ALTITUDE: 1,112M HEIGHT RANK: 41 OS GRID REFERENCE: NH164273

DATE .... TOTAL TIME ....

START TIME .... END TIME ....

DISTANCE .... STEPS ....

STARTING POINT ....

COMPANION(S) ....

....

WEATHER

TEMPERATURE ....

WIND ....

NOTE .... DIFFICULTY ☆☆☆☆☆

....
....
....
....
....

COUNTY: HIGHLAND

SGURR NAN CONBHAIREAN

SECTION / REGION: 11B: GLEN AFFRIC TO GLEN MORISTON

ALTITUDE: 1,109M   HEIGHT RANK: 43   OS GRID REFERENCE: NH129138

DATE .... TOTAL TIME ....

START TIME .... END TIME ....

DISTANCE .... STEPS ....

STARTING POINT ....

COMPANION(S) ....

....

WEATHER

TEMPERATURE
....
WIND ....

NOTE .... DIFFICULTY ☆☆☆☆☆

....
....
....
....
....

COUNTY: HIGHLAND

SGURR MÒR

SECTION / REGION: 14B: THE FANNAICHS

ALTITUDE: 1,108.90M   HEIGHT RANK: 44   OS GRID REFERENCE: NH203718

DATE .... TOTAL TIME ....

START TIME .... END TIME ....

DISTANCE .... STEPS ....

STARTING POINT ....

COMPANION(S) ....

....

WEATHER

TEMPERATURE ....

WIND ....

NOTE .... DIFFICULTY ☆☆☆☆☆

....
....
....
....
....

COUNTY: HIGHLAND

MEALL A' BHUIRIDH

SECTION / REGION: 03C: GLEN ETIVE TO GLEN LOCHY

ALTITUDE: 1,107.90M   HEIGHT RANK: 45   OS GRID REFERENCE: NN250503

DATE .... TOTAL TIME ....

START TIME .... END TIME ....

DISTANCE .... STEPS ....

STARTING POINT ....

COMPANION(S) ....

....

WEATHER

TEMPERATURE
....
WIND ....

NOTE .... DIFFICULTY ☆☆☆☆☆

....
....
....
....
....

COUNTY: HIGHLAND

STOB A' CHOIRE MHEADHOIN

SECTION / REGION: 04A: FORT WILLIAM TO LOCH TREIG & LOCH LEVEN

ALTITUDE: 1,105M   HEIGHT RANK: 46   OS GRID REFERENCE: NN316736

DATE .... TOTAL TIME ....

START TIME .... END TIME ....

DISTANCE .... STEPS ....

STARTING POINT ....

COMPANION(S) ....

....

WEATHER

TEMPERATURE ....

WIND ....

NOTE .... DIFFICULTY ☆☆☆☆☆

....
....
....
....
....

COUNTY: HIGHLAND

BEINN EIBHINN

SECTION / REGION: 04B: LOCH TREIG TO LOCH ERICHT

| ALTITUDE: 1,103.30M | HEIGHT RANK: 47 | OS GRID REFERENCE: NN449733 |

DATE .... TOTAL TIME ....

START TIME .... END TIME ....

DISTANCE .... STEPS ....

STARTING POINT ....

COMPANION(S) ....

....

WEATHER

TEMPERATURE ....

WIND ....

NOTE .... DIFFICULTY ☆☆☆☆☆

....
....
....
....
....

COUNTY: HIGHLAND

MULLACH FRAOCH-CHOIRE

SECTION / REGION: 11B: GLEN AFFRIC TO GLEN MORISTON

ALTITUDE: 1,102M   HEIGHT RANK: 49   OS GRID REFERENCE: NH094171

DATE .... TOTAL TIME ....

START TIME .... END TIME ....

DISTANCE .... STEPS ....

STARTING POINT ....

COMPANION(S) ....

....

WEATHER

TEMPERATURE
....
WIND ....

NOTE .... DIFFICULTY ☆☆☆☆☆

....
....
....
....
....

COUNTY: HIGHLAND

CREISE

SECTION / REGION: 03C: GLEN ETIVE TO GLEN LOCHY

| ALTITUDE: 1,099.80M | HEIGHT RANK: 50 | OS GRID REFERENCE: NN238506 |

DATE .... TOTAL TIME ....

START TIME .... END TIME ....

DISTANCE .... STEPS ....

STARTING POINT ....

COMPANION(S) ....

....

WEATHER

TEMPERATURE ....

WIND ....

NOTE .... DIFFICULTY ☆☆☆☆☆

....
....
....
....
....

COUNTY: HIGHLAND

SGURR A' MHAIM

SECTION / REGION: 04A: FORT WILLIAM TO LOCH TREIG & LOCH LEVEN

ALTITUDE: 1,099M   HEIGHT RANK: 51   OS GRID REFERENCE: NN164667

DATE .... TOTAL TIME ....

START TIME .... END TIME ....

DISTANCE .... STEPS ....

STARTING POINT ....

COMPANION(S) ....

....

WEATHER

TEMPERATURE ....

WIND ....

NOTE .... DIFFICULTY ☆☆☆☆☆

....
....
....
....
....

COUNTY: HIGHLAND

SGURR CHOINNICH MÒR

SECTION / REGION: 04A: FORT WILLIAM TO LOCH TREIG & LOCH LEVEN

| ALTITUDE: 1,094M | HEIGHT RANK: 52 | OS GRID REFERENCE: NN227714 |

DATE .... TOTAL TIME ....

START TIME .... END TIME ....

DISTANCE .... STEPS ....

STARTING POINT ....

COMPANION(S) ....

....

WEATHER

TEMPERATURE ....

WIND ....

NOTE .... DIFFICULTY ☆☆☆☆☆

....
....
....
....
....

COUNTY: HIGHLAND

SGURR NAN CLACH GEALA

SECTION / REGION: 14B: THE FANNAICHS

ALTITUDE: 1,093M   HEIGHT RANK: 53   OS GRID REFERENCE: NH184714

DATE .... TOTAL TIME ....

START TIME .... END TIME ....

DISTANCE .... STEPS ....

STARTING POINT ....

COMPANION(S) ....

....

WEATHER

TEMPERATURE ....

WIND ....

NOTE .... DIFFICULTY ☆☆☆☆☆

....
....
....
....
....

COUNTY: HIGHLAND

BYNACK MORE

SECTION / REGION: 08A: CAIRNGORMS

ALTITUDE: 1,090M   HEIGHT RANK: 55   OS GRID REFERENCE: NJ041063

DATE .... TOTAL TIME ....

START TIME .... END TIME ....

DISTANCE .... STEPS ....

STARTING POINT ....

COMPANION(S) ....

....

WEATHER

TEMPERATURE ....

WIND ....

NOTE .... DIFFICULTY ☆☆☆☆☆

....

....

....

....

COUNTY: HIGHLAND

BEINN A' CHLACHAIR

SECTION / REGION: 04B: LOCH TREIG TO LOCH ERICHT

ALTITUDE: 1,087M   HEIGHT RANK: 56   OS GRID REFERENCE: NN471781

DATE .... TOTAL TIME ....

START TIME .... END TIME ....

DISTANCE .... STEPS ....

STARTING POINT ....

COMPANION(S) ....

....

WEATHER

TEMPERATURE ....

WIND ....

NOTE .... DIFFICULTY ☆☆☆☆☆

....
....
....
....
....

COUNTY: HIGHLAND

BEINN DEARG

SECTION / REGION: 15A: LOCH BROOM TO STRATH OYKEL

| ALTITUDE: 1,084M | HEIGHT RANK: 57 | OS GRID REFERENCE: NH259811 |

DATE .... TOTAL TIME ....

START TIME .... END TIME ....

DISTANCE .... STEPS ....

STARTING POINT ....

COMPANION(S) ....

....

WEATHER

TEMPERATURE ....

WIND ....

NOTE .... DIFFICULTY ☆☆☆☆☆

....
....
....
....
....

COUNTY: HIGHLAND

SGURR A' CHOIRE GHLAIS

SECTION / REGION: 12A: KYLE OF LOCHALSH TO GARVE

| ALTITUDE: 1,083M | HEIGHT RANK: 58 | OS GRID REFERENCE: NH258430 |

DATE .... TOTAL TIME ....

START TIME .... END TIME ....

DISTANCE .... STEPS ....

STARTING POINT ....

COMPANION(S) ....

....

WEATHER

TEMPERATURE ....

WIND ....

NOTE .... DIFFICULTY ☆☆☆☆☆

....

....

....

....

....

COUNTY: HIGHLAND

BEN STARAV

SECTION / REGION: 03C: GLEN ETIVE TO GLEN LOCHY

ALTITUDE: 1,079.50M   HEIGHT RANK: 62   OS GRID REFERENCE: NN125427

DATE .... TOTAL TIME ....

START TIME .... END TIME ....

DISTANCE .... STEPS ....

STARTING POINT ....

COMPANION(S) ....

....

WEATHER

TEMPERATURE
....
WIND ....

NOTE .... DIFFICULTY ☆☆☆☆☆

....
....
....
....
....

COUNTY: HIGHLAND

BIDEAN NAM BIAN - STOB COIRE SGREAMHACH

SECTION / REGION: 03B: LOCH LINNHE TO LOCH ETIVE

ALTITUDE: 1,072M   HEIGHT RANK: 65   OS GRID REFERENCE: NN154536

DATE .... TOTAL TIME ....

START TIME .... END TIME ....

DISTANCE .... STEPS ....

STARTING POINT ....

COMPANION(S) ....

....

WEATHER

TEMPERATURE
....

WIND ....

NOTE .... DIFFICULTY ☆☆☆☆☆

....
....
....
....
....

COUNTY: HIGHLAND

AN SOCACH

SECTION / REGION: 12B: KILLILAN TO INVERNESS

| ALTITUDE: 1,069M | HEIGHT RANK: 67 | OS GRID REFERENCE: NH100332 |

DATE .... TOTAL TIME ....

START TIME .... END TIME ....

DISTANCE .... STEPS ....

STARTING POINT ....

COMPANION(S) ....

....

WEATHER

TEMPERATURE ....

WIND ....

NOTE .... DIFFICULTY ☆☆☆☆☆

....
....
....
....
....

COUNTY: HIGHLAND

SGURR FHUARAN

SECTION / REGION: 11A: LOCH DUICH TO CANNICH

ALTITUDE: 1,068.80M   HEIGHT RANK: 69   OS GRID REFERENCE: NG978166

DATE .... TOTAL TIME ....

START TIME .... END TIME ....

DISTANCE .... STEPS ....

STARTING POINT ....

COMPANION(S) ....

....

WEATHER

☀ ☁ ⛅ 🌧 ⛈ ❄
○ ○ ○ ○ ○ ○

TEMPERATURE
....
WIND ....

NOTE .... DIFFICULTY ☆☆☆☆☆

....
....
....
....
....

COUNTY: HIGHLAND

AN TEALLACH - BIDEIN A' GHLAS THUILL

SECTION / REGION: 14A: LOCH MAREE TO LOCH BROOM

| ALTITUDE: 1,062.50M | HEIGHT RANK: 72 | OS GRID REFERENCE: NH068843 |

DATE .... TOTAL TIME ....

START TIME .... END TIME ....

DISTANCE .... STEPS ....

STARTING POINT ....

COMPANION(S) ....

....

WEATHER

TEMPERATURE ....

WIND ....

NOTE .... DIFFICULTY ☆☆☆☆☆☆

....
....
....
....
....

COUNTY: HIGHLAND

AN TEALLACH - SGURR FIONA

SECTION / REGION: 14A: LOCH MAREE TO LOCH BROOM

ALTITUDE: 1,058.70M   HEIGHT RANK: 73   OS GRID REFERENCE: NH064836

DATE .... TOTAL TIME ....

START TIME .... END TIME ....

DISTANCE .... STEPS ....

STARTING POINT ....

COMPANION(S) ....

....

WEATHER

TEMPERATURE ....

WIND ....

NOTE .... DIFFICULTY ☆☆☆☆☆

....
....
....
....
....

COUNTY: HIGHLAND

LIATHACH - SPIDEAN A' CHOIRE LEITH

SECTION / REGION: 13A: LOCH TORRIDON TO LOCH MAREE

ALTITUDE: 1,054.80M HEIGHT RANK: 74 OS GRID REFERENCE: NG929579

DATE .... TOTAL TIME ....

START TIME .... END TIME ....

DISTANCE .... STEPS ....

STARTING POINT ....

COMPANION(S) ....

....

WEATHER

TEMPERATURE
....
WIND ....

NOTE .... DIFFICULTY ☆☆☆☆☆

COUNTY: HIGHLAND

NA GRUAGAICHEAN

SECTION / REGION: 04A: FORT WILLIAM TO LOCH TREIG & LOCH LEVEN

ALTITUDE: 1,054.30M   HEIGHT RANK: 75   OS GRID REFERENCE: NN203652

DATE .... TOTAL TIME ....

START TIME .... END TIME ....

DISTANCE .... STEPS ....

STARTING POINT ....

COMPANION(S) ....

....

WEATHER

TEMPERATURE ....

WIND ....

NOTE .... DIFFICULTY ☆☆☆☆☆

....
....
....
....
....

COUNTY: HIGHLAND

TOLL CREAGACH

SECTION / REGION: 11A: LOCH DUICH TO CANNICH

ALTITUDE: 1,054M HEIGHT RANK: 76 OS GRID REFERENCE: NH194282

DATE .... TOTAL TIME ....

START TIME .... END TIME ....

DISTANCE .... STEPS ....

STARTING POINT ....

COMPANION(S) ....

....

WEATHER

TEMPERATURE ....

WIND ....

NOTE .... DIFFICULTY ☆☆☆☆☆

....

....

....

....

....

COUNTY: HIGHLAND

STOB POITE COIRE ARDAIR

SECTION / REGION: 09C: LOCH LOCHY TO LOCH LAGGAN

| ALTITUDE: 1,054M | HEIGHT RANK: 77 | OS GRID REFERENCE: NN428888 |

DATE .... TOTAL TIME ....

START TIME .... END TIME ....

DISTANCE .... STEPS ....

STARTING POINT ....

COMPANION(S) ....

....

WEATHER

TEMPERATURE ....

WIND ....

NOTE .... DIFFICULTY ☆☆☆☆☆

....
....
....
....
....

COUNTY: HIGHLAND

SGURR A' CHAORACHAIN

SECTION / REGION: 12A: KYLE OF LOCHALSH TO GARVE

ALTITUDE: 1,053M   HEIGHT RANK: 78   OS GRID REFERENCE: NH087447

DATE .... TOTAL TIME ....

START TIME .... END TIME ....

DISTANCE .... STEPS ....

STARTING POINT ....

COMPANION(S) ....

....

WEATHER

TEMPERATURE
....

WIND ....

NOTE .... DIFFICULTY ☆☆☆☆☆

COUNTY: HIGHLAND

BEINN A' CHAORAINN

SECTION / REGION: 09C: LOCH LOCHY TO LOCH LAGGAN

ALTITUDE: 1,049.10M   HEIGHT RANK: 80   OS GRID REFERENCE: NN386850

DATE .... TOTAL TIME ....

START TIME .... END TIME ....

DISTANCE .... STEPS ....

STARTING POINT ....

COMPANION(S) ....

....

WEATHER

TEMPERATURE
....

WIND ....

NOTE .... DIFFICULTY ☆☆☆☆☆

....
....
....
....
....

COUNTY: HIGHLAND

GEAL CHARN

SECTION / REGION: 04B: LOCH TREIG TO LOCH ERICHT

ALTITUDE: 1,049M   **HEIGHT RANK: 81**   **OS GRID REFERENCE: NN504811**

DATE .... TOTAL TIME ....

START TIME .... END TIME ....

DISTANCE .... STEPS ....

STARTING POINT ....

COMPANION(S) ....

....

WEATHER

TEMPERATURE ....

WIND ....

NOTE .... DIFFICULTY ☆☆☆☆☆

....
....
....
....
....

COUNTY: HIGHLAND

SGURR FHUAR-THUILL

SECTION / REGION: 12A: KYLE OF LOCHALSH TO GARVE

ALTITUDE: 1,049M   HEIGHT RANK: 82   OS GRID REFERENCE: NH235437

DATE .... TOTAL TIME ....

START TIME .... END TIME ....

DISTANCE .... STEPS ....

STARTING POINT ....

COMPANION(S) ....

....

WEATHER

TEMPERATURE ....

WIND ....

NOTE .... DIFFICULTY ☆☆☆☆☆

....

....

....

....

....

COUNTY: HIGHLAND

BEN WYVIS

SECTION / REGION: 15B: LOCH VAICH TO MORAY FIRTH

| ALTITUDE: 1,046M | HEIGHT RANK: 85 | OS GRID REFERENCE: NH462683 |

DATE .... TOTAL TIME ....

START TIME .... END TIME ....

DISTANCE .... STEPS ....

STARTING POINT ....

COMPANION(S) ....

....

WEATHER

TEMPERATURE
....
WIND ....

NOTE .... DIFFICULTY ☆☆☆☆☆

....
....
....
....
....

COUNTY: HIGHLAND

CHNO DEARG

SECTION / REGION: 04B: LOCH TREIG TO LOCH ERICHT

ALTITUDE: 1,046M　　HEIGHT RANK: 86　　OS GRID REFERENCE: NN377741

DATE .... TOTAL TIME ....

START TIME .... END TIME ....

DISTANCE .... STEPS ....

STARTING POINT ....

COMPANION(S) ....

....

WEATHER

TEMPERATURE
....

WIND ....

NOTE .... DIFFICULTY ☆☆☆☆☆

....
....
....
....
....

COUNTY: HIGHLAND

SGÙRR NA CÌCHE

SECTION / REGION: 10B: KNOYDART TO GLEN KINGIE

| ALTITUDE: 1,040.20M | HEIGHT RANK: 92 | OS GRID REFERENCE: NM902966 |

DATE .... TOTAL TIME ....

START TIME .... END TIME ....

DISTANCE .... STEPS ....

STARTING POINT ....

COMPANION(S) ....

....

WEATHER

TEMPERATURE ....

WIND ....

NOTE .... DIFFICULTY ☆☆☆☆☆

....
....
....
....
....

COUNTY: HIGHLAND

SGURR A' BHEALAICH DHEIRG

SECTION / REGION: 11A: LOCH DUICH TO CANNICH

ALTITUDE: 1,036M HEIGHT RANK: 96 OS GRID REFERENCE: NH035143

DATE .... TOTAL TIME ....

START TIME .... END TIME ....

DISTANCE .... STEPS ....

STARTING POINT ....

COMPANION(S) ....

....

WEATHER

TEMPERATURE ....

WIND ....

NOTE .... DIFFICULTY ☆☆☆☆☆

....
....
....
....
....

COUNTY: HIGHLAND

GLEOURAICH

SECTION / REGION: 10A: GLEN SHIEL TO LOCH HOURN AND LOCH QUOICH

ALTITUDE: 1,035M   HEIGHT RANK: 97   OS GRID REFERENCE: NH039053

DATE .... TOTAL TIME ....

START TIME .... END TIME ....

DISTANCE .... STEPS ....

STARTING POINT ....

COMPANION(S) ....

....

WEATHER

TEMPERATURE
....
WIND ....

NOTE .... DIFFICULTY ☆☆☆☆☆

....
....
....
....
....

COUNTY: HIGHLAND

CÀRN DEARG

SECTION / REGION: 04B: LOCH TREIG TO LOCH ERICHT

ALTITUDE: 1,034M   HEIGHT RANK: 98   OS GRID REFERENCE: NN504764

DATE .... TOTAL TIME ....

START TIME .... END TIME ....

DISTANCE .... STEPS ....

STARTING POINT ....

COMPANION(S) ....

....

WEATHER

TEMPERATURE ....

WIND ....

NOTE .... DIFFICULTY ☆☆☆☆☆

....
....
....
....
....

COUNTY: HIGHLAND

BEINN FHADA (BEN ATTOW)

SECTION / REGION: 11A: LOCH DUICH TO CANNICH

ALTITUDE: 1,031.90M HEIGHT RANK: 99 OS GRID REFERENCE: NH018192

DATE .... TOTAL TIME ....

START TIME .... END TIME ....

DISTANCE .... STEPS ....

STARTING POINT ....

COMPANION(S) ....

....

WEATHER

TEMPERATURE
....
WIND ....

NOTE .... DIFFICULTY ☆☆☆☆☆

....
....
....
....
....

COUNTY: HIGHLAND

AM BODACH

SECTION / REGION: 04A: FORT WILLIAM TO LOCH TREIG & LOCH LEVEN

ALTITUDE: 1,031.80M   HEIGHT RANK: 100   OS GRID REFERENCE: NN176650

DATE .... TOTAL TIME ....

START TIME .... END TIME ....

DISTANCE .... STEPS ....

STARTING POINT ....

COMPANION(S) ....

....

WEATHER

TEMPERATURE ....

WIND ....

NOTE .... DIFFICULTY ☆☆☆☆☆

....
....
....
....
....

COUNTY: HIGHLAND

SGURR A' MHAORAICH

SECTION / REGION: 10A: GLEN SHIEL TO LOCH HOURN AND LOCH QUOICH

ALTITUDE: 1,027M   HEIGHT RANK: 104   OS GRID REFERENCE: NG983065

DATE .... TOTAL TIME ....

START TIME .... END TIME ....

DISTANCE .... STEPS ....

STARTING POINT ....

COMPANION(S) ....

....

WEATHER

TEMPERATURE
....
WIND ....

NOTE .... DIFFICULTY ☆☆☆☆☆

....
....
....
....
....

COUNTY: HIGHLAND

SGURR NA CISTE DUIBHE

SECTION / REGION: 11A: LOCH DUICH TO CANNICH

ALTITUDE: 1,027M   HEIGHT RANK: 105   OS GRID REFERENCE: NG984149

DATE .... TOTAL TIME ....

START TIME .... END TIME ....

DISTANCE .... STEPS ....

STARTING POINT ....

COMPANION(S) ....

....

WEATHER

TEMPERATURE ....

WIND ....

NOTE .... DIFFICULTY ☆☆☆☆☆

....
....
....
....
....

COUNTY: HIGHLAND

BEINN A' BHEITHIR - SGORR DHEARG

SECTION / REGION: 03B: LOCH LINNHE TO LOCH ETIVE

| ALTITUDE: 1,024M | HEIGHT RANK: 107 | OS GRID REFERENCE: NN056558 |

DATE .... TOTAL TIME ....

START TIME .... END TIME ....

DISTANCE .... STEPS ....

STARTING POINT ....

COMPANION(S) ....

....

WEATHER

TEMPERATURE ....

WIND ....

NOTE .... DIFFICULTY ☆☆☆☆☆

....
....
....
....
....

COUNTY: HIGHLAND

LIATHACH - MULLACH AN RATHAIN

SECTION / REGION: 13A: LOCH TORRIDON TO LOCH MAREE

ALTITUDE: 1,023.80M HEIGHT RANK: 108 OS GRID REFERENCE: NG911576

DATE .... TOTAL TIME ....

START TIME .... END TIME ....

DISTANCE .... STEPS ....

STARTING POINT ....

COMPANION(S) ....

....

WEATHER

TEMPERATURE ....

WIND ....

NOTE .... DIFFICULTY ☆☆☆☆☆

....

....

....

....

....

COUNTY: HIGHLAND

BUACHAILLE ETIVE MÒR - STOB DEARG

SECTION / REGION: 03B: LOCH LINNHE TO LOCH ETIVE

ALTITUDE: 1,021.40M HEIGHT RANK: 109 OS GRID REFERENCE: NN222542

DATE .... TOTAL TIME ....

START TIME .... END TIME ....

DISTANCE .... STEPS ....

STARTING POINT ....

COMPANION(S) ....

....

WEATHER

TEMPERATURE
....
WIND ....

NOTE .... DIFFICULTY ☆☆☆☆☆

....
....
....
....
....

COUNTY: HIGHLAND

LADHAR BHEINN

SECTION / REGION: 10B: KNOYDART TO GLEN KINGIE

ALTITUDE: 1,020M   HEIGHT RANK: 110   OS GRID REFERENCE: NG824039

DATE .... TOTAL TIME ....

START TIME .... END TIME ....

DISTANCE .... STEPS ....

STARTING POINT ....

COMPANION(S) ....

....

WEATHER

TEMPERATURE ....

WIND ....

NOTE .... DIFFICULTY ☆☆☆☆☆

....
....
....
....
....

COUNTY: HIGHLAND

AONACH AIR CHRITH

SECTION / REGION: 10A: GLEN SHIEL TO LOCH HOURN AND LOCH QUOICH

ALTITUDE: 1,019.50M HEIGHT RANK: 111 OS GRID REFERENCE: NH051083

DATE .... TOTAL TIME ....

START TIME .... END TIME ....

DISTANCE .... STEPS ....

STARTING POINT ....

COMPANION(S) ....

....

WEATHER

TEMPERATURE ....

WIND ....

NOTE .... DIFFICULTY ☆☆☆☆☆

COUNTY: HIGHLAND

BEINN BHEOIL

SECTION / REGION: 04B: LOCH TREIG TO LOCH ERICHT

ALTITUDE: 1,019M   HEIGHT RANK: 112   OS GRID REFERENCE: NN517717

DATE .... TOTAL TIME ....

START TIME .... END TIME ....

DISTANCE .... STEPS ....

STARTING POINT ....

COMPANION(S) ....

....

WEATHER

TEMPERATURE ....

WIND ....

NOTE .... DIFFICULTY ☆☆☆☆☆

....

....

....

....

....

COUNTY: HIGHLAND

MULLACH CLACH A' BHLAIR

SECTION / REGION: 08A: CAIRNGORMS

ALTITUDE: 1,019M HEIGHT RANK: 113 OS GRID REFERENCE: NN882927

DATE .... TOTAL TIME ....

START TIME .... END TIME ....

DISTANCE .... STEPS ....

STARTING POINT ....

COMPANION(S) ....

....

WEATHER

TEMPERATURE
....
WIND ....

NOTE .... DIFFICULTY ☆☆☆☆☆

....
....
....
....
....

COUNTY: HIGHLAND

MULLACH COIRE MHIC FHEARCHAIR

SECTION / REGION: 14A: LOCH MAREE TO LOCH BROOM

ALTITUDE: 1,015.20M   HEIGHT RANK: 115   OS GRID REFERENCE: NH052735

DATE .... TOTAL TIME ....

START TIME .... END TIME ....

DISTANCE .... STEPS ....

STARTING POINT ....

COMPANION(S) ....

....

WEATHER

TEMPERATURE ....

WIND ....

NOTE .... DIFFICULTY ☆☆☆☆☆

....
....
....
....
....

COUNTY: HIGHLAND

GARBH CHIOCH MHÒR

SECTION / REGION: 10B: KNOYDART TO GLEN KINGIE

ALTITUDE: 1,012.90M HEIGHT RANK: 116 OS GRID REFERENCE: NM909961

DATE .... TOTAL TIME ....

START TIME .... END TIME ....

DISTANCE .... STEPS ....

STARTING POINT ....

COMPANION(S) ....

....

WEATHER

TEMPERATURE
....
WIND ....

NOTE .... DIFFICULTY ☆☆☆☆☆

....
....
....
....
....

COUNTY: HIGHLAND

THE SADDLE (AN DÌOLLAID)

SECTION / REGION: 10A: GLEN SHIEL TO LOCH HOURN AND LOCH QUOICH

ALTITUDE: 1,011.50M HEIGHT RANK: 119 OS GRID REFERENCE: NG936131

DATE .... TOTAL TIME ....

START TIME .... END TIME ....

DISTANCE .... STEPS ....

STARTING POINT ....

COMPANION(S) ....

....

WEATHER

TEMPERATURE ....

WIND ....

NOTE .... DIFFICULTY ☆☆☆☆☆

....
....
....
....
....

COUNTY: HIGHLAND

BEINN EIGHE - RUADH-STAC MÒR

SECTION / REGION: 13A: LOCH TORRIDON TO LOCH MAREE

| ALTITUDE: 1,010M | HEIGHT RANK: 121 | OS GRID REFERENCE: NG951611 |

DATE .... TOTAL TIME ....

START TIME .... END TIME ....

DISTANCE .... STEPS ....

STARTING POINT ....

COMPANION(S) ....

....

WEATHER

TEMPERATURE
....

WIND ....

NOTE .... DIFFICULTY ☆☆☆☆☆

COUNTY: HIGHLAND

SGURR EILDE MÒR

SECTION / REGION: 04A: FORT WILLIAM TO LOCH TREIG & LOCH LEVEN

ALTITUDE: 1,010M HEIGHT RANK: 122 OS GRID REFERENCE: NN230657

DATE .... TOTAL TIME ....

START TIME .... END TIME ....

DISTANCE .... STEPS ....

STARTING POINT ....

COMPANION(S) ....

....

WEATHER

TEMPERATURE ....

WIND ....

NOTE .... DIFFICULTY ☆☆☆☆☆

....
....
....
....
....

COUNTY: HIGHLAND

SGURR AN DOIRE LEATHAIN

SECTION / REGION: 10A: GLEN SHIEL TO LOCH HOURN AND LOCH QUOICH

ALTITUDE: 1,010M HEIGHT RANK: 123 OS GRID REFERENCE: NH015098

DATE .... TOTAL TIME ....

START TIME .... END TIME ....

DISTANCE .... STEPS ....

STARTING POINT ....

COMPANION(S) ....

....

WEATHER

TEMPERATURE ....

WIND ....

NOTE .... DIFFICULTY ☆☆☆☆☆

....
....
....
....
....

COUNTY: HIGHLAND

CÀRN LIATH

SECTION / REGION: 09C: LOCH LOCHY TO LOCH LAGGAN

ALTITUDE: 1,006M HEIGHT RANK: 127 OS GRID REFERENCE: NN472903

DATE .... TOTAL TIME ....

START TIME .... END TIME ....

DISTANCE .... STEPS ....

STARTING POINT ....

COMPANION(S) ....

....

WEATHER

TEMPERATURE ....

WIND ....

NOTE .... DIFFICULTY ☆☆☆☆☆

....
....
....
....
....

COUNTY: HIGHLAND

MAOILE LUNNDAIDH

SECTION / REGION: 12A: KYLE OF LOCHALSH TO GARVE

ALTITUDE: 1,004.90M HEIGHT RANK: 128 OS GRID REFERENCE: NH135458

DATE .... TOTAL TIME ....

START TIME .... END TIME ....

DISTANCE .... STEPS ....

STARTING POINT ....

COMPANION(S) ....

....

WEATHER

TEMPERATURE ....

WIND ....

NOTE .... DIFFICULTY ☆☆☆☆☆

....
....
....
....
....

COUNTY: HIGHLAND

BEINN FHIONNLAIDH

SECTION / REGION: 11A: LOCH DUICH TO CANNICH

ALTITUDE: 1,004.80M HEIGHT RANK: 129 OS GRID REFERENCE: NH115282

DATE .... TOTAL TIME ....

START TIME .... END TIME ....

DISTANCE .... STEPS ....

STARTING POINT ....

COMPANION(S) ....

....

WEATHER

TEMPERATURE ....

WIND ....

NOTE .... DIFFICULTY ☆☆☆☆☆

....
....
....
....
....

COUNTY: HIGHLAND

SGURR AN LOCHAIN

SECTION / REGION: 10A: GLEN SHIEL TO LOCH HOURN AND LOCH QUOICH

ALTITUDE: 1,004M HEIGHT RANK: 131 OS GRID REFERENCE: NH005104

DATE .... TOTAL TIME ....

START TIME .... END TIME ....

DISTANCE .... STEPS ....

STARTING POINT ....

COMPANION(S) ....

....

WEATHER

TEMPERATURE
....

WIND ....

NOTE .... DIFFICULTY ☆☆☆☆☆

COUNTY: HIGHLAND

SGURR MOR

SECTION / REGION: 10B: KNOYDART TO GLEN KINGIE

ALTITUDE: 1,003M   HEIGHT RANK: 132   OS GRID REFERENCE: NM965980

DATE .... TOTAL TIME ....

START TIME .... END TIME ....

DISTANCE .... STEPS ....

STARTING POINT ....

COMPANION(S) ....

....

WEATHER

TEMPERATURE ....

WIND ....

NOTE .... DIFFICULTY ☆☆☆☆☆

....

....

....

....

....

COUNTY: HIGHLAND

SGURR NA CARNACH

SECTION / REGION: 11A: LOCH DUICH TO CANNICH

ALTITUDE: 1,002M   HEIGHT RANK: 133   OS GRID REFERENCE: NG977158

DATE .... TOTAL TIME ....

START TIME .... END TIME ....

DISTANCE .... STEPS ....

STARTING POINT ....

COMPANION(S) ....

....

WEATHER

TEMPERATURE
....
WIND ....

NOTE .... DIFFICULTY ☆☆☆☆☆

....
....
....
....
....

COUNTY: HIGHLAND

BEINN A' BHEITHIR - SGORR DHONUILL

SECTION / REGION: 03B: LOCH LINNHE TO LOCH ETIVE

ALTITUDE: 1,001M   HEIGHT RANK: 134   OS GRID REFERENCE: NN040555

DATE .... TOTAL TIME ....

START TIME .... END TIME ....

DISTANCE .... STEPS ....

STARTING POINT ....

COMPANION(S) ....

....

WEATHER

TEMPERATURE
....
WIND ....

NOTE .... DIFFICULTY ☆☆☆☆☆

....
....
....
....
....

COUNTY: HIGHLAND

AONACH MEADHOIN

SECTION / REGION: 11A: LOCH DUICH TO CANNICH

ALTITUDE: 1,001M   HEIGHT RANK: 135   OS GRID REFERENCE: NH048137

DATE .... TOTAL TIME ....

START TIME................................. END TIME ....

DISTANCE................................... STEPS ....

STARTING POINT ....

COMPANION(S) ....

....

WEATHER   TEMPERATURE
                                    ....
                                    WIND ....

NOTE .... DIFFICULTY ☆☆☆☆☆

....
....
....
....
....

COUNTY: HIGHLAND

STOB BÀN

SECTION / REGION: 04A: FORT WILLIAM TO LOCH TREIG & LOCH LEVEN

ALTITUDE: 999.7M   HEIGHT RANK: 137   OS GRID REFERENCE: NN147654

DATE .... TOTAL TIME ....

START TIME .... END TIME ....

DISTANCE .... STEPS ....

STARTING POINT ....

COMPANION(S) ....

....

WEATHER

TEMPERATURE ....

WIND ....

NOTE .... DIFFICULTY ☆☆☆☆☆

....
....
....
....
....

COUNTY: HIGHLAND

SGURR BREAC

SECTION / REGION: 14B: THE FANNAICHS

ALTITUDE: 999.6M　　HEIGHT RANK: 138　　OS GRID REFERENCE: NH158711

DATE .... TOTAL TIME ....

START TIME .... END TIME ....

DISTANCE .... STEPS ....

STARTING POINT ....

COMPANION(S) ....

....

WEATHER

TEMPERATURE
....
WIND ....

NOTE .... DIFFICULTY ☆☆☆☆☆

....
....
....
....
....

COUNTY: HIGHLAND

SGURR CHOINNICH

SECTION / REGION: 12A: KYLE OF LOCHALSH TO GARVE

ALTITUDE: 999.3M   HEIGHT RANK: 139   OS GRID REFERENCE: NH076446

DATE .... TOTAL TIME ....

START TIME .... END TIME ....

DISTANCE .... STEPS ....

STARTING POINT ....

COMPANION(S) ....

....

WEATHER

TEMPERATURE ....

WIND ....

NOTE .... DIFFICULTY ☆☆☆☆☆

....

....

....

....

....

COUNTY: HIGHLAND

SAIL CHAORAINN

SECTION / REGION: 11B: GLEN AFFRIC TO GLEN MORISTON

| ALTITUDE: 999.2M | HEIGHT RANK: 141 | OS GRID REFERENCE: NH133154 |

DATE .... TOTAL TIME ....

START TIME................................. END TIME ....

DISTANCE.................................... STEPS ....

STARTING POINT ....

COMPANION(S) ....

....

WEATHER

TEMPERATURE
....
WIND ....

NOTE .... DIFFICULTY ☆☆☆☆☆

....
....
....
....
....

COUNTY: HIGHLAND

A' CHAILLEACH

SECTION / REGION: 14B: THE FANNAICHS

ALTITUDE: 998.6M	HEIGHT RANK: 142	OS GRID REFERENCE: NH136714

DATE .... TOTAL TIME ....

START TIME................................ END TIME ....

DISTANCE.................................... STEPS ....

STARTING POINT ....

COMPANION(S) ....

....

WEATHER

TEMPERATURE ....

WIND ....

NOTE .... DIFFICULTY ☆☆☆☆☆

....

....

....

....

....

COUNTY: HIGHLAND

BEN MORE ASSYNT

SECTION / REGION: 16E: SCOURIE TO LAIRG

ALTITUDE: 998M   HEIGHT RANK: 143   OS GRID REFERENCE: NC318201

DATE .... TOTAL TIME ....

START TIME .... END TIME ....

DISTANCE .... STEPS ....

STARTING POINT ....

COMPANION(S) ....

....

WEATHER

TEMPERATURE ....

WIND ....

NOTE .... DIFFICULTY ☆☆☆☆☆

....
....
....
....
....

COUNTY: HIGHLAND

SPIDEAN MIALACH

SECTION / REGION: 10A: GLEN SHIEL TO LOCH HOURN AND LOCH QUOICH

ALTITUDE: 996M　　HEIGHT RANK: 146　　OS GRID REFERENCE: NH065043

DATE .... TOTAL TIME ....

START TIME............................ END TIME ....

DISTANCE.............................. STEPS ....

STARTING POINT ....

COMPANION(S) ....

....

WEATHER

TEMPERATURE
....

WIND ....

NOTE .... DIFFICULTY ☆☆☆☆☆

....

....

....

....

....

COUNTY: HIGHLAND

SGURR NA H-ULAIDH

SECTION / REGION: 03B: LOCH LINNHE TO LOCH ETIVE

ALTITUDE: 994M	HEIGHT RANK: 148	OS GRID REFERENCE: NN111517

DATE .... TOTAL TIME ....

START TIME................................. END TIME ....

DISTANCE.................................... STEPS ....

STARTING POINT ....

COMPANION(S) ....

....

WEATHER

TEMPERATURE ....

WIND ....

NOTE .... DIFFICULTY ☆☆☆☆☆

....

....

....

....

....

COUNTY: HIGHLAND

SGURR NA RUAIDHE

SECTION / REGION: 12A: KYLE OF LOCHALSH TO GARVE

ALTITUDE: 993M   HEIGHT RANK: 150   OS GRID REFERENCE: NH289426

DATE .... TOTAL TIME ....

START TIME.................................. END TIME ....

DISTANCE..................................... STEPS ....

STARTING POINT ....

COMPANION(S) ....

....

WEATHER

TEMPERATURE ....

WIND ....

NOTE .... DIFFICULTY ☆☆☆☆☆

....

....

....

....

....

COUNTY: HIGHLAND

CÀRN NAN GOBHAR (MULLARDOCH)

SECTION / REGION: 12B: KILLILAN TO INVERNESS

ALTITUDE: 993M   HEIGHT RANK: 151   OS GRID REFERENCE: NH181343

DATE .... TOTAL TIME ....

START TIME .... END TIME ....

DISTANCE .... STEPS ....

STARTING POINT ....

COMPANION(S) ....

....

WEATHER

TEMPERATURE ....

WIND ....

NOTE .... DIFFICULTY ☆☆☆☆☆

....
....
....
....
....

COUNTY: HIGHLAND

BEINN EIGHE - SPIDEAN COIRE NAN CLACH

SECTION / REGION: 13A: LOCH TORRIDON TO LOCH MAREE

ALTITUDE: 993M	HEIGHT RANK: 152	OS GRID REFERENCE: NG966597

DATE .... TOTAL TIME ....

START TIME .... END TIME ....

DISTANCE .... STEPS ....

STARTING POINT ....

COMPANION(S) ....

....

WEATHER

TEMPERATURE ....

WIND ....

NOTE .... DIFFICULTY ☆☆☆☆☆

....
....
....
....
....

COUNTY: HIGHLAND

SGÙRR ALASDAIR

SECTION / REGION: 17B: MINGINISH AND THE CUILLIN HILLS

ALTITUDE: 992M	HEIGHT RANK: 153	OS GRID REFERENCE: NG450207

DATE .... TOTAL TIME ....

START TIME .... END TIME ....

DISTANCE .... STEPS ....

STARTING POINT ....

COMPANION(S) ....

....

WEATHER

TEMPERATURE ....

WIND ....

NOTE .... DIFFICULTY ☆☆☆☆☆

....
....
....
....
....

COUNTY: HIGHLAND

CÀRN NAN GOBHAR (STRATHFARRAR)

SECTION / REGION: 12A: KYLE OF LOCHALSH TO GARVE

ALTITUDE: 992M   HEIGHT RANK: 154   OS GRID REFERENCE: NH273438

DATE .... TOTAL TIME ....

START TIME .... END TIME ....

DISTANCE .... STEPS ....

STARTING POINT ....

COMPANION(S) ....

....

WEATHER

TEMPERATURE ....

WIND ....

NOTE .... DIFFICULTY ☆☆☆☆☆

....
....
....
....
....

COUNTY: HIGHLAND

SGURR BÀN

SECTION / REGION: 14A: LOCH MAREE TO LOCH BROOM

ALTITUDE: 989M HEIGHT RANK: 157 OS GRID REFERENCE: NH055745

DATE .... TOTAL TIME ....

START TIME .... END TIME ....

DISTANCE .... STEPS ....

STARTING POINT ....

COMPANION(S) ....

....

WEATHER

TEMPERATURE ....

WIND ....

NOTE .... DIFFICULTY ☆☆☆☆☆

....
....
....
....
....

COUNTY: HIGHLAND

GAOR BHEINN (GULVAIN)

SECTION / REGION: 10D: MALLAIG TO FORT WILLIAM

ALTITUDE: 987M   HEIGHT RANK: 159   OS GRID REFERENCE: NN002875

DATE .... TOTAL TIME ....

START TIME................................. END TIME ....

DISTANCE.................................... STEPS ....

STARTING POINT ....

COMPANION(S) ....

....

WEATHER

☀ ☁ ⛅ 🌧 ⛈ ❄
● ● ● ● ● ●

TEMPERATURE
....
WIND ....

NOTE .... DIFFICULTY ☆☆☆☆☆

....
....
....
....
....

COUNTY: HIGHLAND

LURG MHÒR

SECTION / REGION: 12A: KYLE OF LOCHALSH TO GARVE

| ALTITUDE: 987M | HEIGHT RANK: 160 | OS GRID REFERENCE: NH064404 |

DATE .... TOTAL TIME ....

START TIME................................. END TIME ....

DISTANCE.................................... STEPS ....

STARTING POINT ....

COMPANION(S) ....

....

WEATHER

TEMPERATURE ....

WIND ....

NOTE .... DIFFICULTY ☆☆☆☆☆

....
....
....
....
....

COUNTY: HIGHLAND

CONIVAL

SECTION / REGION: 16E: SCOURIE TO LAIRG

ALTITUDE: 987M   HEIGHT RANK: 161   OS GRID REFERENCE: NC303199

DATE .... TOTAL TIME ....

START TIME .... END TIME ....

DISTANCE .... STEPS ....

STARTING POINT ....

COMPANION(S) ....

....

WEATHER

☀ ☁ ⛅ 🌧 ⛈ ❄
○ ○ ○ ○ ○ ○

TEMPERATURE
....
WIND ....

NOTE .... DIFFICULTY ☆☆☆☆☆

....
....
....
....
....

COUNTY: HIGHLAND

BEINN ALLIGIN - SGÙRR MHÒR

SECTION / REGION: 13A: LOCH TORRIDON TO LOCH MAREE

ALTITUDE: 986M	HEIGHT RANK: 162	OS GRID REFERENCE: NG865612

DATE .... TOTAL TIME ....

START TIME .... END TIME ....

DISTANCE .... STEPS ....

STARTING POINT ....

COMPANION(S) ....

....

WEATHER ☀️ ☁️ ⛅ 🌧️ ⛈️ ❄️

TEMPERATURE ....

WIND ....

NOTE .... DIFFICULTY ☆☆☆☆☆

....

....

....

....

....

COUNTY: HIGHLAND

SGÙRR DEARG (INACCESSIBLE PINNACLE)

SECTION / REGION: 17B: MINGINISH AND THE CUILLIN HILLS

| ALTITUDE: 985.8M | HEIGHT RANK: 163 | OS GRID REFERENCE: NG444215 |

DATE .... TOTAL TIME ....

START TIME............................ END TIME ....

DISTANCE............................... STEPS ....

STARTING POINT ....

COMPANION(S) ....

....

WEATHER

TEMPERATURE ....

WIND ....

NOTE .... DIFFICULTY ☆☆☆☆☆

....

....

....

....

....

COUNTY: HIGHLAND

DRUIM SHIONNACH

SECTION / REGION: 10A: GLEN SHIEL TO LOCH HOURN AND LOCH QUOICH

| ALTITUDE: 985.2M | HEIGHT RANK: 165 | OS GRID REFERENCE: NH074084 |

DATE .... TOTAL TIME ....

START TIME .... END TIME ....

DISTANCE .... STEPS ....

STARTING POINT ....

COMPANION(S) ....

....

WEATHER

TEMPERATURE ....

WIND ....

NOTE .... DIFFICULTY ☆☆☆☆☆

....
....
....
....
....

COUNTY: HIGHLAND

MULLACH NA DHEIRAGAIN

SECTION / REGION: 11A: LOCH DUICH TO CANNICH

ALTITUDE: 982M   HEIGHT RANK: 166   OS GRID REFERENCE: NH080259

DATE .... TOTAL TIME ....

START TIME.................................. END TIME ....

DISTANCE..................................... STEPS ....

STARTING POINT ....

COMPANION(S) ....

....

WEATHER

TEMPERATURE ....

WIND ....

NOTE .... DIFFICULTY ☆☆☆☆☆

....
....
....
....
....

COUNTY: HIGHLAND

AN GEARANACH

SECTION / REGION: 04A: FORT WILLIAM TO LOCH TREIG & LOCH LEVEN

ALTITUDE: 981.5M   HEIGHT RANK: 167   OS GRID REFERENCE: NN187669

DATE .... TOTAL TIME ....

START TIME .... END TIME ....

DISTANCE .... STEPS ....

STARTING POINT ....

COMPANION(S) ....

....

WEATHER

TEMPERATURE
....
WIND ....

NOTE .... DIFFICULTY ☆☆☆☆☆

....
....
....
....
....

COUNTY: HIGHLAND

STOB COIRE A' CHAIRN

SECTION / REGION: 04A: FORT WILLIAM TO LOCH TREIG & LOCH LEVEN

| ALTITUDE: 981.3M | HEIGHT RANK: 168 | OS GRID REFERENCE: NN185660 |

DATE .... TOTAL TIME ....

START TIME................................ END TIME ....

DISTANCE.................................... STEPS ....

STARTING POINT ....

COMPANION(S) ....

....

WEATHER

TEMPERATURE ....

WIND ....

NOTE .... DIFFICULTY ☆☆☆☆☆

....

....

....

....

....

COUNTY: HIGHLAND

CISTE DHUBH

SECTION / REGION: 11A: LOCH DUICH TO CANNICH

ALTITUDE: 981.1M   HEIGHT RANK: 169   OS GRID REFERENCE: NH062166

DATE .... TOTAL TIME ....

START TIME .... END TIME ....

DISTANCE .... STEPS ....

STARTING POINT ....

COMPANION(S) ....

....

WEATHER

TEMPERATURE
....

WIND ....

NOTE .... DIFFICULTY ☆☆☆☆☆

....

....

....

....

....

COUNTY: HIGHLAND

SLIOCH

SECTION / REGION: 14A: LOCH MAREE TO LOCH BROOM

| ALTITUDE: 981M | HEIGHT RANK: 170 | OS GRID REFERENCE: NH004690 |

DATE .... TOTAL TIME ....

START TIME .... END TIME ....

DISTANCE .... STEPS ....

STARTING POINT ....

COMPANION(S) ....

....

WEATHER

TEMPERATURE ....

WIND ....

NOTE .... DIFFICULTY ☆☆☆☆☆

....

....

....

....

....

COUNTY: HIGHLAND

MAOL CHINN-DEARG

SECTION / REGION: 10A: GLEN SHIEL TO LOCH HOURN AND LOCH QUOICH

| ALTITUDE: 980.3M | HEIGHT RANK: 172 | OS GRID REFERENCE: NH032087 |

DATE .... TOTAL TIME ....

START TIME .... END TIME ....

DISTANCE .... STEPS ....

STARTING POINT ....

COMPANION(S) ....

....

WEATHER

TEMPERATURE ....

WIND ....

NOTE .... DIFFICULTY ☆☆☆☆☆

COUNTY: HIGHLAND

STOB COIRE SGRIODAIN

SECTION / REGION: 04B: LOCH TREIG TO LOCH ERICHT

ALTITUDE: 979M HEIGHT RANK: 174 OS GRID REFERENCE: NN356743

DATE .... TOTAL TIME ....

START TIME .... END TIME ....

DISTANCE .... STEPS ....

STARTING POINT ....

COMPANION(S) ....

....

WEATHER

TEMPERATURE ....

WIND ....

NOTE .... DIFFICULTY ☆☆☆☆☆

....
....
....
....
....

COUNTY: HIGHLAND

CONA' MHEALL

SECTION / REGION: 15A: LOCH BROOM TO STRATH OYKEL

ALTITUDE: 978M   HEIGHT RANK: 176   OS GRID REFERENCE: NH275816

DATE .... TOTAL TIME ....

START TIME .... END TIME ....

DISTANCE .... STEPS ....

STARTING POINT ....

COMPANION(S) ....

....

WEATHER

TEMPERATURE
....
WIND ....

NOTE .... DIFFICULTY ☆☆☆☆☆

....

....

....

....

....

COUNTY: HIGHLAND

STOB BÀN

SECTION / REGION: 04A: FORT WILLIAM TO LOCH TREIG & LOCH LEVEN

| ALTITUDE: 977M | HEIGHT RANK: 177 | OS GRID REFERENCE: NN266723 |

DATE .... TOTAL TIME ....

START TIME................................. END TIME ....

DISTANCE..................................... STEPS ....

STARTING POINT ....

COMPANION(S) ....

....

WEATHER

TEMPERATURE ....

WIND ....

NOTE .... DIFFICULTY ☆☆☆☆☆

....

....

....

....

....

COUNTY: HIGHLAND

MEALL NAN CEAPRAICHEAN

SECTION / REGION: 15A: LOCH BROOM TO STRATH OYKEL

| ALTITUDE: 977M | HEIGHT RANK: 178 | OS GRID REFERENCE: NH257825 |

DATE .... TOTAL TIME ....

START TIME................................... END TIME ....

DISTANCE...................................... STEPS ....

STARTING POINT ....

COMPANION(S) ....

....

WEATHER

TEMPERATURE
....
WIND ....

NOTE .... DIFFICULTY ☆☆☆☆☆

....

....

....

....

....

COUNTY: HIGHLAND

BEINN SGRITHEALL

SECTION / REGION: 10A: GLEN SHIEL TO LOCH HOURN AND LOCH QUOICH

ALTITUDE: 974M   HEIGHT RANK: 181   OS GRID REFERENCE: NG835126

DATE .... TOTAL TIME ....

START TIME .... END TIME ....

DISTANCE .... STEPS ....

STARTING POINT ....

COMPANION(S) ....

....

WEATHER

TEMPERATURE ....

WIND ....

NOTE .... DIFFICULTY ☆☆☆☆☆

....

....

....

....

....

COUNTY: HIGHLAND

A' MHARCONAICH

SECTION / REGION: 05A: LOCH ERICHT TO GLEN TROMIE & GLEN GARRY

| ALTITUDE: 973.2M | HEIGHT RANK: 183 | OS GRID REFERENCE: NN604762 |

DATE .... TOTAL TIME ....

START TIME .... END TIME ....

DISTANCE .... STEPS ....

STARTING POINT ....

COMPANION(S) ....

....

WEATHER

TEMPERATURE ....

WIND ....

NOTE .... DIFFICULTY ☆☆☆☆☆

....
....
....
....
....

COUNTY: HIGHLAND

SGURR A' GHREADAIDH

SECTION / REGION: 17B: MINGINISH AND THE CUILLIN HILLS

ALTITUDE: 972.1M HEIGHT RANK: 185 OS GRID REFERENCE: NG445231

DATE .... TOTAL TIME ....

START TIME .... END TIME ....

DISTANCE .... STEPS ....

STARTING POINT ....

COMPANION(S) ....

....

WEATHER

TEMPERATURE ....

WIND ....

NOTE .... DIFFICULTY ☆☆☆☆☆

....
....
....
....
....

COUNTY: HIGHLAND

AONACH EAGACH - SGORR NAM FIANNAIDH

SECTION / REGION: 03A: LOCH LEVEN TO RANNOCH STATION

ALTITUDE: 967.7M   HEIGHT RANK: 187   OS GRID REFERENCE: NN140583

DATE .... TOTAL TIME ....

START TIME .... END TIME ....

DISTANCE .... STEPS ....

STARTING POINT ....

COMPANION(S) ....

....

WEATHER

TEMPERATURE ....

WIND ....

NOTE .... DIFFICULTY ☆☆☆☆☆

....
....
....
....
....

COUNTY: HIGHLAND

A' MHAIGHDEAN

SECTION / REGION: 14A: LOCH MAREE TO LOCH BROOM

| ALTITUDE: 967M | HEIGHT RANK: 188 | OS GRID REFERENCE: NH007749 |

DATE .... TOTAL TIME ....

START TIME .... END TIME ....

DISTANCE .... STEPS ....

STARTING POINT ....

COMPANION(S) ....

....

WEATHER

☀ ☁ ⛅ 🌧 ⛈ ❄

TEMPERATURE ....

WIND ....

NOTE .... DIFFICULTY ☆☆☆☆☆

....

....

....

....

....

COUNTY: HIGHLAND

SGÙRR NAN GILLEAN

SECTION / REGION: 17B: MINGINISH AND THE CUILLIN HILLS

| ALTITUDE: 966.1M | HEIGHT RANK: 189 | OS GRID REFERENCE: NG471253 |

DATE .... TOTAL TIME ....

START TIME .... END TIME ....

DISTANCE .... STEPS ....

STARTING POINT ....

COMPANION(S) ....

....

WEATHER

TEMPERATURE
....
WIND ....

NOTE .... DIFFICULTY ☆☆☆☆☆

....
....
....
....
....

COUNTY: HIGHLAND

SGURR NA BANACHDAICH

SECTION / REGION: 17B: MINGINISH AND THE CUILLIN HILLS

ALTITUDE: 965M   HEIGHT RANK: 191   OS GRID REFERENCE: NG440224

DATE .... TOTAL TIME ....

START TIME .... END TIME ....

DISTANCE .... STEPS ....

STARTING POINT ....

COMPANION(S) ....

....

WEATHER

TEMPERATURE ....

WIND ....

NOTE .... DIFFICULTY ☆☆☆☆☆

....
....
....
....
....

COUNTY: HIGHLAND

SGURR THUILM

SECTION / REGION: 10D: MALLAIG TO FORT WILLIAM

ALTITUDE: 963M   HEIGHT RANK: 193   OS GRID REFERENCE: NM939879

DATE .... TOTAL TIME ....

START TIME .... END TIME ....

DISTANCE .... STEPS ....

STARTING POINT ....

COMPANION(S) ....

....

WEATHER

TEMPERATURE ....

WIND ....

NOTE .... DIFFICULTY ☆☆☆☆☆

....
....
....
....
....

COUNTY: HIGHLAND

BEN KILBRECK - MEALL NAN CON

SECTION / REGION: 16D: ALTNAHARRA TO DORNOCH

ALTITUDE: 962.1M   HEIGHT RANK: 194   OS GRID REFERENCE: NC585299

DATE .... TOTAL TIME ....

START TIME .... END TIME ....

DISTANCE .... STEPS ....

STARTING POINT ....

COMPANION(S) ....

....

WEATHER

TEMPERATURE ....

WIND ....

NOTE .... DIFFICULTY ☆☆☆☆☆

....

....

....

....

....

COUNTY: HIGHLAND

SGORR RUADH

SECTION / REGION: 13B: APPLECROSS TO ACHNASHEEN

ALTITUDE: 960.7M   HEIGHT RANK: 195   OS GRID REFERENCE: NG959505

DATE .... TOTAL TIME ....

START TIME .... END TIME ....

DISTANCE .... STEPS ....

STARTING POINT ....

COMPANION(S) ....

....

WEATHER

TEMPERATURE ....

WIND ....

NOTE .... DIFFICULTY ☆☆☆☆☆

....
....
....
....
....

COUNTY: HIGHLAND

BRUACH NA FRITHE

SECTION / REGION: 17B: MINGINISH AND THE CUILLIN HILLS

| ALTITUDE: 958.8M | HEIGHT RANK: 200 | OS GRID REFERENCE: NG460252 |

DATE .... TOTAL TIME ....

START TIME .... END TIME ....

DISTANCE .... STEPS ....

STARTING POINT ....

COMPANION(S) ....

....

WEATHER

TEMPERATURE ....

WIND ....

NOTE .... DIFFICULTY ☆☆☆☆☆

....

....

....

....

....

COUNTY: HIGHLAND

BUACHAILLE ETIVE BEAG - STOB DUBH

SECTION / REGION: 03B: LOCH LINNHE TO LOCH ETIVE

ALTITUDE: 958M   HEIGHT RANK: 201   OS GRID REFERENCE: NN179535

DATE .... TOTAL TIME ....

START TIME .... END TIME ....

DISTANCE .... STEPS ....

STARTING POINT ....

COMPANION(S) ....

....

WEATHER

TEMPERATURE
....
WIND ....

NOTE .... DIFFICULTY ☆☆☆☆☆

....
....
....
....
....

COUNTY: HIGHLAND

CÀRN GHLUASAID

SECTION / REGION: 11B: GLEN AFFRIC TO GLEN MORISTON

ALTITUDE: 957M	HEIGHT RANK: 204	OS GRID REFERENCE: NH145125

DATE .... TOTAL TIME ....

START TIME............................ END TIME ....

DISTANCE................................ STEPS ....

STARTING POINT ....

COMPANION(S) ....

....

WEATHER

TEMPERATURE ....

WIND ....

NOTE .... DIFFICULTY ☆☆☆☆☆

....
....
....
....
....

COUNTY: HIGHLAND

SGURR NAN COIREACHAN

SECTION / REGION: 10D: MALLAIG TO FORT WILLIAM

| ALTITUDE: 956M | HEIGHT RANK: 205 | OS GRID REFERENCE: NM902880 |

DATE .... TOTAL TIME ....

START TIME .... END TIME ....

DISTANCE .... STEPS ....

STARTING POINT ....

COMPANION(S) ....

....

WEATHER

TEMPERATURE
....

WIND ....

NOTE .... DIFFICULTY ☆☆☆☆☆

....
....
....
....
....

COUNTY: HIGHLAND

SAILEAG

SECTION / REGION: 11A: LOCH DUICH TO CANNICH

ALTITUDE: 956M   HEIGHT RANK: 206   OS GRID REFERENCE: NH017148

DATE .... TOTAL TIME ....

START TIME .... END TIME ....

DISTANCE .... STEPS ....

STARTING POINT ....

COMPANION(S) ....

....

WEATHER

TEMPERATURE ....

WIND ....

NOTE .... DIFFICULTY ☆☆☆☆☆

....
....
....
....
....

COUNTY: HIGHLAND

BEINN LIATH MHÒR FANNAICH

SECTION / REGION: 14B: THE FANNAICHS

ALTITUDE: 954M   HEIGHT RANK: 208   OS GRID REFERENCE: NH219724

DATE .... TOTAL TIME ....

START TIME .... END TIME ....

DISTANCE .... STEPS ....

STARTING POINT ....

COMPANION(S) ....

....

WEATHER

TEMPERATURE
....
WIND ....

NOTE .... DIFFICULTY ☆☆☆☆☆

....
....
....
....
....

COUNTY: HIGHLAND

SGURR NAN COIREACHAN

SECTION / REGION: 10B: KNOYDART TO GLEN KINGIE

ALTITUDE: 953.8M HEIGHT RANK: 209 OS GRID REFERENCE: NM933958

DATE .... TOTAL TIME ....

START TIME .... END TIME ....

DISTANCE .... STEPS ....

STARTING POINT ....

COMPANION(S) ....

....

WEATHER

TEMPERATURE
....
WIND ....

NOTE .... DIFFICULTY ☆☆☆☆☆

....
....
....
....
....

COUNTY: HIGHLAND

BUACHAILLE ETIVE MÒR - STOB NA BRÒIGE

SECTION / REGION: 03B: LOCH LINNHE TO LOCH ETIVE

ALTITUDE: 953.4M HEIGHT RANK: 210 OS GRID REFERENCE: NN190525

DATE .... TOTAL TIME ....

START TIME .... END TIME ....

DISTANCE .... STEPS ....

STARTING POINT ....

COMPANION(S) ....

....

WEATHER

TEMPERATURE
....
WIND ....

NOTE .... DIFFICULTY ☆☆☆☆☆

....
....
....
....
....

COUNTY: HIGHLAND

AM FAOCHAGACH

SECTION / REGION: 15A: LOCH BROOM TO STRATH OYKEL

ALTITUDE: 953M   HEIGHT RANK: 212   OS GRID REFERENCE: NH303793

DATE .... TOTAL TIME ....

START TIME............................ END TIME ....

DISTANCE............................... STEPS ....

STARTING POINT ....

COMPANION(S) ....

....

WEATHER

TEMPERATURE
....

WIND ....

NOTE .... DIFFICULTY ☆☆☆☆☆

....

....

....

....

....

COUNTY: HIGHLAND

AONACH EAGACH - MEALL DEARG

SECTION / REGION: 03A: LOCH LEVEN TO RANNOCH STATION

| ALTITUDE: 952.3M | HEIGHT RANK: 213 | OS GRID REFERENCE: NN161583 |

DATE .... TOTAL TIME ....

START TIME .... END TIME ....

DISTANCE .... STEPS ....

STARTING POINT ....

COMPANION(S) ....

....

WEATHER

TEMPERATURE ....

WIND ....

NOTE .... DIFFICULTY ☆☆☆☆☆

....
....
....
....
....

COUNTY: HIGHLAND

MEALL CHUAICH

SECTION / REGION: 05B: LOCH ERICHT TO GLEN TROMIE & GLEN GARRY

ALTITUDE: 951M HEIGHT RANK: 214 OS GRID REFERENCE: NN716878

DATE .... TOTAL TIME ....

START TIME................................. END TIME ....

DISTANCE..................................... STEPS ....

STARTING POINT ....

COMPANION(S) ....

....

WEATHER

TEMPERATURE ....

WIND ....

NOTE .... DIFFICULTY ☆☆☆☆☆

....
....
....
....
....

COUNTY: HIGHLAND

MEALL GORM

SECTION / REGION: 14B: THE FANNAICHS

ALTITUDE: 949.7M	HEIGHT RANK: 215	OS GRID REFERENCE: NH221695

DATE .... TOTAL TIME ....

START TIME .... END TIME ....

DISTANCE .... STEPS ....

STARTING POINT ....

COMPANION(S) ....

....

WEATHER

TEMPERATURE
....
WIND ....

NOTE .... DIFFICULTY ☆☆☆☆☆

....

....

....

....

....

COUNTY: HIGHLAND

SGURR MHIC CHOINNICH

SECTION / REGION: 17B: MINGINISH AND THE CUILLIN HILLS

ALTITUDE: 948.1M   HEIGHT RANK: 217   OS GRID REFERENCE: NG450210

DATE .... TOTAL TIME ....

START TIME............................ END TIME ....

DISTANCE.............................. STEPS ....

STARTING POINT ....

COMPANION(S) ....

....

WEATHER

TEMPERATURE
....

WIND ....

NOTE .... DIFFICULTY ☆☆☆☆☆

....
....
....
....
....

COUNTY: HIGHLAND

CREAG A' MHAIM

SECTION / REGION: 10A: GLEN SHIEL TO LOCH HOURN AND LOCH QUOICH

ALTITUDE: 946.2M   HEIGHT RANK: 219   OS GRID REFERENCE: NH087077

DATE .... TOTAL TIME ....

START TIME .... END TIME ....

DISTANCE .... STEPS ....

STARTING POINT ....

COMPANION(S) ....

....

WEATHER

TEMPERATURE ....

WIND ....

NOTE .... DIFFICULTY ☆☆☆☆☆

....

....

....

....

....

COUNTY: HIGHLAND

MEALL BUIDHE

SECTION / REGION: 10B: KNOYDART TO GLEN KINGIE

ALTITUDE: 946M   HEIGHT RANK: 220   OS GRID REFERENCE: NM848989

DATE .... TOTAL TIME ....

START TIME .... END TIME ....

DISTANCE .... STEPS ....

STARTING POINT ....

COMPANION(S) ....

....

WEATHER

TEMPERATURE
....
WIND ....

NOTE .... DIFFICULTY ☆☆☆☆☆

....
....
....
....
....

COUNTY: HIGHLAND

SGURR NA SGINE

SECTION / REGION: 10A: GLEN SHIEL TO LOCH HOURN AND LOCH QUOICH

ALTITUDE: 946M	HEIGHT RANK: 221	OS GRID REFERENCE: NG946113

DATE .... TOTAL TIME ....

START TIME .... END TIME ....

DISTANCE .... STEPS ....

STARTING POINT ....

COMPANION(S) ....

....

WEATHER

TEMPERATURE ....

WIND ....

NOTE .... DIFFICULTY ☆☆☆☆☆

....
....
....
....
....

COUNTY: HIGHLAND

CÀRN DEARG

SECTION / REGION: 09B: GLEN ALBYN AND THE MONADH LIATH

ALTITUDE: 945.7M   HEIGHT RANK: 223   OS GRID REFERENCE: NH635023

DATE .... TOTAL TIME ....

START TIME .... END TIME ....

DISTANCE .... STEPS ....

STARTING POINT ....

COMPANION(S) ....

....

WEATHER

TEMPERATURE ....

WIND ....

NOTE .... DIFFICULTY ☆☆☆☆☆

....

....

....

....

....

COUNTY: HIGHLAND

BIDEIN A' CHOIRE SHEASGAICH

SECTION / REGION: 12A: KYLE OF LOCHALSH TO GARVE

ALTITUDE: 945M   HEIGHT RANK: 226   OS GRID REFERENCE: NH049412

DATE .... TOTAL TIME ....

START TIME .... END TIME ....

DISTANCE .... STEPS ....

STARTING POINT ....

COMPANION(S) ....

....

WEATHER

TEMPERATURE
....
WIND ....

NOTE .... DIFFICULTY ☆☆☆☆☆

....
....
....
....
....

COUNTY: HIGHLAND

SGURR DUBH MOR

SECTION / REGION: 17B: MINGINISH AND THE CUILLIN HILLS

ALTITUDE: 944M HEIGHT RANK: 228 OS GRID REFERENCE: NG457205

DATE .... TOTAL TIME ....

START TIME .... END TIME ....

DISTANCE .... STEPS ....

STARTING POINT ....

COMPANION(S) ....

....

WEATHER

TEMPERATURE ....

WIND ....

NOTE .... DIFFICULTY ☆☆☆☆☆

....
....
....
....
....

COUNTY: HIGHLAND

BINNEIN BEAG

SECTION / REGION: 04A: FORT WILLIAM TO LOCH TREIG & LOCH LEVEN

ALTITUDE: 943M   HEIGHT RANK: 230   OS GRID REFERENCE: NN221677

DATE .... TOTAL TIME ....

START TIME................................. END TIME ....

DISTANCE.................................... STEPS ....

STARTING POINT ....

COMPANION(S) ....

....

WEATHER

TEMPERATURE
....
WIND ....

NOTE .... DIFFICULTY ☆☆☆☆☆

....
....
....
....
....

COUNTY: HIGHLAND

MULLACH NAN COIREAN

SECTION / REGION: 04A: FORT WILLIAM TO LOCH TREIG & LOCH LEVEN

ALTITUDE: 939.3M   HEIGHT RANK: 234   OS GRID REFERENCE: NN122662

DATE .... TOTAL TIME ....

START TIME.................................. END TIME ....

DISTANCE..................................... STEPS ....

STARTING POINT ....

COMPANION(S) ....

....

WEATHER   TEMPERATURE
☀ ☁ ⛅ 🌧 ⛈ ❄   ....
● ● ● ● ● ●   WIND ....

NOTE .... DIFFICULTY ☆☆☆☆☆

....
....
....
....
....

COUNTY: HIGHLAND

LUINNE BHEINN

SECTION / REGION: 10B: KNOYDART TO GLEN KINGIE

ALTITUDE: 939M   HEIGHT RANK: 236   OS GRID REFERENCE: NG869007

DATE .... TOTAL TIME ....

START TIME .... END TIME ....

DISTANCE .... STEPS ....

STARTING POINT ....

COMPANION(S) ....

....

WEATHER

TEMPERATURE
....
WIND ....

NOTE .... DIFFICULTY ☆☆☆☆☆

....

....

....

....

....

COUNTY: HIGHLAND

SRON A' CHOIRE GHAIRBH

SECTION / REGION: 10C: LOCH ARKAIG TO GLEN MORISTON

ALTITUDE: 937M HEIGHT RANK: 238 OS GRID REFERENCE: NN222945

DATE .... TOTAL TIME ....

START TIME .... END TIME ....

DISTANCE .... STEPS ....

STARTING POINT ....

COMPANION(S) ....

....

WEATHER

TEMPERATURE ....

WIND ....

NOTE .... DIFFICULTY ☆☆☆☆☆

....

....

....

....

....

COUNTY: HIGHLAND

BEINN NA LAP

SECTION / REGION: 04B: LOCH TREIG TO LOCH ERICHT

| ALTITUDE: 935M | HEIGHT RANK: 240 | OS GRID REFERENCE: NN376695 |

DATE .... TOTAL TIME ....

START TIME .... END TIME ....

DISTANCE .... STEPS ....

STARTING POINT ....

COMPANION(S) ....

....

WEATHER

TEMPERATURE
....
WIND ....

NOTE .... DIFFICULTY ☆☆☆☆☆

....
....
....
....
....

COUNTY: HIGHLAND

MEALL A' CHRASGAIDH

SECTION / REGION: 14B: THE FANNAICHS

ALTITUDE: 934M   HEIGHT RANK: 241   OS GRID REFERENCE: NH184733

DATE .... TOTAL TIME ....

START TIME .... END TIME ....

DISTANCE .... STEPS ....

STARTING POINT ....

COMPANION(S) ....

....

WEATHER

TEMPERATURE ....

WIND ....

NOTE .... DIFFICULTY ☆☆☆☆☆

....

....

....

....

....

COUNTY: HIGHLAND

AM BASTEIR

SECTION / REGION: 17B: MINGINISH AND THE CUILLIN HILLS

| ALTITUDE: 934M | HEIGHT RANK: 242 | OS GRID REFERENCE: NG465253 |

DATE .... TOTAL TIME ....

START TIME .... END TIME ....

DISTANCE .... STEPS ....

STARTING POINT ....

COMPANION(S) ....

....

WEATHER

TEMPERATURE
....
WIND ....

NOTE .... DIFFICULTY ☆☆☆☆☆

....
....
....
....
....

COUNTY: HIGHLAND

BEINN TARSUINN

SECTION / REGION: 14A: LOCH MAREE TO LOCH BROOM

ALTITUDE: 933.8M   HEIGHT RANK: 243   OS GRID REFERENCE: NH039727

DATE .... TOTAL TIME ....

START TIME .... END TIME ....

DISTANCE .... STEPS ....

STARTING POINT ....

COMPANION(S) ....

....

WEATHER

TEMPERATURE ....

WIND ....

NOTE .... DIFFICULTY ☆☆☆☆☆

....
....
....
....
....

COUNTY: HIGHLAND

FIONN BHEINN

SECTION / REGION: 14B: THE FANNAICHS

ALTITUDE: 933M　　HEIGHT RANK: 244　　OS GRID REFERENCE: NH147621

DATE .... TOTAL TIME ....

START TIME .... END TIME ....

DISTANCE .... STEPS ....

STARTING POINT ....

COMPANION(S) ....

....

WEATHER

TEMPERATURE
....
WIND ....

NOTE .... DIFFICULTY ☆☆☆☆☆

....
....
....
....
....

COUNTY: HIGHLAND

MAOL CHEAN-DEARG

SECTION / REGION: 13B: APPLECROSS TO ACHNASHEEN

ALTITUDE: 933M   HEIGHT RANK: 245   OS GRID REFERENCE: NG924499

DATE .... TOTAL TIME ....

START TIME .... END TIME ....

DISTANCE .... STEPS ....

STARTING POINT ....

COMPANION(S) ....

....

WEATHER

TEMPERATURE ....

WIND ....

NOTE .... DIFFICULTY ☆☆☆☆☆

COUNTY: HIGHLAND

A' CHAILLEACH

SECTION / REGION: 09B: GLEN ALBYN AND THE MONADH LIATH

ALTITUDE: 929.3M   HEIGHT RANK: 251   OS GRID REFERENCE: NH681041

DATE .... TOTAL TIME ....

START TIME .... END TIME ....

DISTANCE .... STEPS ....

STARTING POINT ....

COMPANION(S) ....

....

WEATHER

TEMPERATURE ....

WIND ....

NOTE .... DIFFICULTY ☆☆☆☆☆

COUNTY: HIGHLAND

BLÀ BHEINN (BLAVEN)

SECTION / REGION: 17B: MINGINISH AND THE CUILLIN HILLS

ALTITUDE: 929M   HEIGHT RANK: 252   OS GRID REFERENCE: NG529217

DATE .... TOTAL TIME ....

START TIME .... END TIME ....

DISTANCE .... STEPS ....

STARTING POINT ....

COMPANION(S) ....

....

WEATHER

TEMPERATURE ....

WIND ....

NOTE .... DIFFICULTY ☆☆☆☆☆

....
....
....
....
....

COUNTY: HIGHLAND

MORUISG

SECTION / REGION: 12A: KYLE OF LOCHALSH TO GARVE

ALTITUDE: 928M	HEIGHT RANK: 254	OS GRID REFERENCE: NH101499

DATE .... TOTAL TIME ....

START TIME .... END TIME ....

DISTANCE .... STEPS ....

STARTING POINT ....

COMPANION(S) ....

....

WEATHER

TEMPERATURE
....
WIND ....

NOTE .... DIFFICULTY ☆☆☆☆☆

....
....
....
....
....

COUNTY: HIGHLAND

BEN HOPE (BEINN HÒB)

SECTION / REGION: 16B: DURNESS TO LOCH SHIN

ALTITUDE: 927M   HEIGHT RANK: 256   OS GRID REFERENCE: NC477501

DATE .... TOTAL TIME ....

START TIME .... END TIME ....

DISTANCE .... STEPS ....

STARTING POINT ....

COMPANION(S) ....

....

WEATHER

TEMPERATURE ....

WIND ....

NOTE .... DIFFICULTY ☆☆☆☆☆

....
....
....
....
....

COUNTY: HIGHLAND

EIDIDH NAN CLACH GEALA

SECTION / REGION: 15A: LOCH BROOM TO STRATH OYKEL

| ALTITUDE: 927M | HEIGHT RANK: 258 | OS GRID REFERENCE: NH257842 |

DATE .... TOTAL TIME ....

START TIME................................ END TIME ....

DISTANCE.................................... STEPS ....

STARTING POINT ....

COMPANION(S) ....

....

WEATHER

TEMPERATURE ....

WIND ....

NOTE .... DIFFICULTY ☆☆☆☆☆

COUNTY: HIGHLAND

SGURR NAN EAG

SECTION / REGION: 17B: MINGINISH AND THE CUILLIN HILLS

ALTITUDE: 926.3M   HEIGHT RANK: 259   OS GRID REFERENCE: NG457195

DATE .... TOTAL TIME ....

START TIME .... END TIME ....

DISTANCE .... STEPS ....

STARTING POINT ....

COMPANION(S) ....

....

WEATHER

TEMPERATURE
....

WIND ....

NOTE .... DIFFICULTY ☆☆☆☆☆

....

....

....

....

....

COUNTY: HIGHLAND

BEINN LIATH MHÒR

SECTION / REGION: 13B: APPLECROSS TO ACHNASHEEN

ALTITUDE: 926M **HEIGHT RANK:** 260 **OS GRID REFERENCE:** NG964519

DATE .... TOTAL TIME ....

START TIME .... END TIME ....

DISTANCE .... STEPS ....

STARTING POINT ....

COMPANION(S) ....

....

WEATHER

TEMPERATURE ....

WIND ....

NOTE .... DIFFICULTY ☆☆☆☆☆

....
....
....
....
....

COUNTY: HIGHLAND

SEANA BHRAIGH

SECTION / REGION: 15A: LOCH BROOM TO STRATH OYKEL

ALTITUDE: 926M   HEIGHT RANK: 261   OS GRID REFERENCE: NH281878

DATE .... TOTAL TIME ....

START TIME .... END TIME ....

DISTANCE .... STEPS ....

STARTING POINT ....

COMPANION(S) ....

....

WEATHER

TEMPERATURE ....

WIND ....

NOTE .... DIFFICULTY ☆☆☆☆☆

....
....
....
....
....

COUNTY: HIGHLAND

GEAL CHÀRN

SECTION / REGION: 09B: GLEN ALBYN AND THE MONADH LIATH

| ALTITUDE: 926M | HEIGHT RANK: 262 | OS GRID REFERENCE: NN561987 |

DATE .... TOTAL TIME ....

START TIME .... END TIME ....

DISTANCE .... STEPS ....

STARTING POINT ....

COMPANION(S) ....

....

WEATHER

TEMPERATURE
....

WIND ....

NOTE .... DIFFICULTY ☆☆☆☆☆

....

....

....

....

....

COUNTY: HIGHLAND

BUACHAILLE ETIVE BEAG - STOB COIRE RAINEACH

SECTION / REGION: 03B: LOCH LINNHE TO LOCH ETIVE

| ALTITUDE: 924.5M | HEIGHT RANK: 264 | OS GRID REFERENCE: NN191548 |

DATE .... TOTAL TIME ....

START TIME .... END TIME ....

DISTANCE .... STEPS ....

STARTING POINT ....

COMPANION(S) ....

....

WEATHER

TEMPERATURE ....

WIND ....

NOTE .... DIFFICULTY ☆☆☆☆☆

....
....
....
....
....

COUNTY: HIGHLAND

AN COILEACHAN

SECTION / REGION: 14B: THE FANNAICHS

ALTITUDE: 924M   HEIGHT RANK: 265   OS GRID REFERENCE: NH241680

DATE .... TOTAL TIME ....

START TIME .... END TIME ....

DISTANCE .... STEPS ....

STARTING POINT ....

COMPANION(S) ....

....

WEATHER

TEMPERATURE ....

WIND ....

NOTE .... DIFFICULTY ☆☆☆☆☆

COUNTY: HIGHLAND

CREAG PITRIDH

SECTION / REGION: 04B: LOCH TREIG TO LOCH ERICHT

ALTITUDE: 924M   HEIGHT RANK: 266   OS GRID REFERENCE: NN487814

DATE .... TOTAL TIME ....

START TIME .... END TIME ....

DISTANCE .... STEPS ....

STARTING POINT ....

COMPANION(S) ....

....

WEATHER

TEMPERATURE ....

WIND ....

NOTE .... DIFFICULTY ☆☆☆☆☆

....
....
....
....
....

COUNTY: HIGHLAND

SGURR NAN EACH

SECTION / REGION: 14B: THE FANNAICHS

ALTITUDE: 923M　　HEIGHT RANK: 267　　OS GRID REFERENCE: NH184697

DATE .... TOTAL TIME ....

START TIME .... END TIME ....

DISTANCE .... STEPS ....

STARTING POINT ....

COMPANION(S) ....

....

WEATHER

TEMPERATURE ....

WIND ....

NOTE .... DIFFICULTY ☆☆☆☆☆

....
....
....
....
....

COUNTY: HIGHLAND

BEINN ALLIGIN - TOM NA GRUAGAICH

SECTION / REGION: 13A: LOCH TORRIDON TO LOCH MAREE

ALTITUDE: 922M	HEIGHT RANK: 268	OS GRID REFERENCE: NG859601

DATE .... TOTAL TIME ....

START TIME .... END TIME ....

DISTANCE..................................... STEPS ....

STARTING POINT ....

COMPANION(S) ....

....

WEATHER

☀ ☁ ⛅ 🌧 ⛈ ❄
● ● ● ● ● ●

TEMPERATURE
....
WIND ....

NOTE .... DIFFICULTY ☆☆☆☆☆

....
....
....
....
....

COUNTY: HIGHLAND

CARN SGULAIN

SECTION / REGION: 09B: GLEN ALBYN AND THE MONADH LIATH

ALTITUDE: 920.3M　　HEIGHT RANK: 269　　OS GRID REFERENCE: NH683058

DATE .... TOTAL TIME ....

START TIME .... END TIME ....

DISTANCE .... STEPS ....

STARTING POINT ....

COMPANION(S) ....

....

WEATHER

TEMPERATURE ....

WIND ....

NOTE .... DIFFICULTY ☆☆☆☆☆

....
....
....
....
....

COUNTY: HIGHLAND

AN SOCACH

SECTION / REGION: 11A: LOCH DUICH TO CANNICH

ALTITUDE: 919.7M　　HEIGHT RANK: 271　　OS GRID REFERENCE: NH088229

DATE .... TOTAL TIME ....

START TIME .... END TIME ....

DISTANCE .... STEPS ....

STARTING POINT ....

COMPANION(S) ....

....

WEATHER

☀ ☁ ⛅ 🌧 ⛈ ❄

● ● ● ● ● ●

TEMPERATURE ....

WIND ....

NOTE .... DIFFICULTY ☆☆☆☆☆

....
....
....
....
....

COUNTY: HIGHLAND

GAIRICH

SECTION / REGION: 10B: KNOYDART TO GLEN KINGIE

| ALTITUDE: 919M | HEIGHT RANK: 272 | OS GRID REFERENCE: NN025995 |

DATE .... TOTAL TIME ....

START TIME .... END TIME ....

DISTANCE .... STEPS ....

STARTING POINT ....

COMPANION(S) ....

....

WEATHER

TEMPERATURE ....

WIND ....

NOTE .... DIFFICULTY ☆☆☆☆☆

....
....
....
....
....

COUNTY: HIGHLAND

RUADH STAC MOR

SECTION / REGION: 14A: LOCH MAREE TO LOCH BROOM

ALTITUDE: 918.7M　　HEIGHT RANK: 273　　OS GRID REFERENCE: NH018756

DATE .... TOTAL TIME ....

START TIME .... END TIME ....

DISTANCE .... STEPS ....

STARTING POINT ....

COMPANION(S) ....

....

WEATHER

TEMPERATURE ....

WIND ....

NOTE .... DIFFICULTY ☆☆☆☆☆

....
....
....
....
....

COUNTY: HIGHLAND

A' GHLAS-BHEINN

SECTION / REGION: 11A: LOCH DUICH TO CANNICH

| ALTITUDE: 918M | HEIGHT RANK: 274 | OS GRID REFERENCE: NH008231 |

DATE .... TOTAL TIME ....

START TIME .... END TIME ....

DISTANCE .... STEPS ....

STARTING POINT ....

COMPANION(S) ....

....

WEATHER

TEMPERATURE
....
WIND ....

NOTE .... DIFFICULTY ☆☆☆☆☆

....
....
....
....
....

COUNTY: HIGHLAND

SGURR A' MHADAIDH

SECTION / REGION: 17B: MINGINISH AND THE CUILLIN HILLS

ALTITUDE: 918M   HEIGHT RANK: 275   OS GRID REFERENCE: NG446235

DATE .... TOTAL TIME ....

START TIME .... END TIME ....

DISTANCE .... STEPS ....

STARTING POINT ....

COMPANION(S) ....

....

WEATHER

TEMPERATURE ....

WIND ....

NOTE .... DIFFICULTY ☆☆☆☆☆

....
....
....
....
....

COUNTY: HIGHLAND

CREAG NAN DAMH

SECTION / REGION: 10A: GLEN SHIEL TO LOCH HOURN AND LOCH QUOICH

ALTITUDE: 917.2M   HEIGHT RANK: 276   OS GRID REFERENCE: NG983112

DATE .... TOTAL TIME ....

START TIME .... END TIME ....

DISTANCE .... STEPS ....

STARTING POINT ....

COMPANION(S) ....

....

WEATHER

TEMPERATURE
....
WIND ....

NOTE .... DIFFICULTY ☆☆☆☆☆

....
....
....
....
....

COUNTY: HIGHLAND

GEAL-CHÀRN

SECTION / REGION: 05A: LOCH ERICHT TO GLEN TROMIE & GLEN GARRY

ALTITUDE: 917.1M   HEIGHT RANK: 277   OS GRID REFERENCE: NN596782

DATE .... TOTAL TIME ....

START TIME .... END TIME ....

DISTANCE .... STEPS ....

STARTING POINT ....

COMPANION(S) ....

....

WEATHER

TEMPERATURE
....
WIND ....

NOTE .... DIFFICULTY ☆☆☆☆☆

....

....

....

....

....

COUNTY: HIGHLAND

MEALL NA TEANGA

SECTION / REGION: 10C: LOCH ARKAIG TO GLEN MORISTON

| ALTITUDE: 916.8M | HEIGHT RANK: 278 | OS GRID REFERENCE: NN220924 |

DATE .... TOTAL TIME ....

START TIME .... END TIME ....

DISTANCE .... STEPS ....

STARTING POINT ....

COMPANION(S) ....

....

WEATHER

TEMPERATURE ....

WIND ....

NOTE .... DIFFICULTY ☆☆☆☆☆

....
....
....
....
....

COUNTY: HIGHLAND

BEINN TEALLACH

SECTION / REGION: 09C: LOCH LOCHY TO LOCH LAGGAN

ALTITUDE: 914.6M   HEIGHT RANK: 282   OS GRID REFERENCE: NN361859

DATE .... TOTAL TIME ....

START TIME .... END TIME ....

DISTANCE .... STEPS ....

STARTING POINT ....

COMPANION(S) ....

....

WEATHER

TEMPERATURE
....
WIND ....

NOTE .... DIFFICULTY ☆☆☆☆☆

....
....
....
....
....

COUNTY: HIGHLAND / MORAY

CAIRN GORM (AN CÀRN GORM)

SECTION / REGION: 08A: CAIRNGORMS

| ALTITUDE: 1,244.80M | HEIGHT RANK: 6 | OS GRID REFERENCE: NJ005040 |

DATE .... TOTAL TIME ....

START TIME .... END TIME ....

DISTANCE .... STEPS ....

STARTING POINT ....

COMPANION(S) ....

....

WEATHER

TEMPERATURE
....
WIND ....

NOTE .... DIFFICULTY ☆☆☆☆☆

....
....
....
....
....

COUNTY: HIGHLAND / PERTH AND KINROSS

BEINN UDLAMAIN

SECTION / REGION: 05A: LOCH ERICHT TO GLEN TROMIE & GLEN GARRY

ALTITUDE: 1,010.20M   HEIGHT RANK: 120   OS GRID REFERENCE: NN579739

DATE .... TOTAL TIME ....

START TIME .... END TIME ....

DISTANCE .... STEPS ....

STARTING POINT ....

COMPANION(S) ....

....

WEATHER

TEMPERATURE ....

WIND ....

NOTE .... DIFFICULTY ☆☆☆☆☆

....
....
....
....
....

COUNTY: HIGHLAND/ PERTH AND KINROSS

SGOR GAIBHRE

SECTION / REGION: 04B: LOCH TREIG TO LOCH ERICHT

ALTITUDE: 955M	HEIGHT RANK: 207	OS GRID REFERENCE: NN444674

DATE .... TOTAL TIME ....

START TIME .... END TIME ....

DISTANCE .... STEPS ....

STARTING POINT ....

COMPANION(S) ....

....

WEATHER

TEMPERATURE ....

WIND ....

NOTE .... DIFFICULTY ☆☆☆☆☆

....

....

....

....

....

COUNTY: HIGHLAND / PERTH AND KINROSS

CARN DEARG

SECTION / REGION: 04B: LOCH TREIG TO LOCH ERICHT

ALTITUDE: 941M   HEIGHT RANK: 232   OS GRID REFERENCE: NN417661

DATE .... TOTAL TIME ....

START TIME .... END TIME ....

DISTANCE .... STEPS ....

STARTING POINT ....

COMPANION(S) ....

....

WEATHER

TEMPERATURE ....

WIND ....

NOTE .... DIFFICULTY ☆☆☆☆☆

....
....
....
....
....

COUNTY: HIGHLAND / PERTH AND KINROSS

CÀRN NA CAIM

SECTION / REGION: 05B: LOCH ERICHT TO GLEN TROMIE & GLEN GARRY

ALTITUDE: 940.8M	HEIGHT RANK: 233	OS GRID REFERENCE: NN677821

DATE .... TOTAL TIME ....

START TIME .... END TIME ....

DISTANCE .... STEPS ....

STARTING POINT ....

COMPANION(S) ....

....

WEATHER

TEMPERATURE
....

WIND ....

NOTE .... DIFFICULTY ☆☆☆☆☆

....

....

....

....

....

COUNTY: HIGHLAND / PERTH AND KINROSS

A' BHUIDHEANACH BHEAG

SECTION / REGION: 05B: LOCH ERICHT TO GLEN TROMIE & GLEN GARRY

ALTITUDE: 936.1M   HEIGHT RANK: 239   OS GRID REFERENCE: NN660775

DATE .... TOTAL TIME ....

START TIME .... END TIME ....

DISTANCE .... STEPS ....

STARTING POINT ....

COMPANION(S) ....

....

WEATHER

TEMPERATURE
....
WIND ....

NOTE .... DIFFICULTY ☆☆☆☆☆

....

....

....

....

....

COUNTY: MORAY

BEINN MHEADHOIN

SECTION / REGION: 08A: CAIRNGORMS

ALTITUDE: 1,182.90M   HEIGHT RANK: 12   OS GRID REFERENCE: NJ024016

DATE .... TOTAL TIME ....

START TIME .... END TIME ....

DISTANCE .... STEPS ....

STARTING POINT ....

COMPANION(S) ....

....

WEATHER

TEMPERATURE ....

WIND ....

NOTE .... DIFFICULTY ☆☆☆☆☆

....
....
....
....
....

COUNTY: PERTH AND KINROSS

BEN LAWERS (BEINN LABHAIR)

SECTION / REGION: 02B: GLEN LYON TO GLEN DOCHART & LOCH TAY

| ALTITUDE: 1,214M | HEIGHT RANK: 10 | OS GRID REFERENCE: NN635414 |

DATE .... TOTAL TIME ....

START TIME .... END TIME ....

DISTANCE .... STEPS ....

STARTING POINT ....

COMPANION(S) ....

....

WEATHER

TEMPERATURE ....

WIND ....

NOTE .... DIFFICULTY ☆☆☆☆☆

....
....
....
....
....

COUNTY: PERTH AND KINROSS

MEALL GARBH

SECTION / REGION: 02B: GLEN LYON TO GLEN DOCHART & LOCH TAY

ALTITUDE: 1,123.10M   HEIGHT RANK: 32   OS GRID REFERENCE: NN644437

DATE .... TOTAL TIME ....

START TIME .... END TIME ....

DISTANCE .... STEPS ....

STARTING POINT ....

COMPANION(S) ....

....

WEATHER

TEMPERATURE ....

WIND ....

NOTE .... DIFFICULTY ☆☆☆☆☆

....
....
....
....
....

COUNTY: PERTH AND KINROSS

BEINN A' GHLÓ - CÀRN NAN GABHAR

SECTION / REGION: 06B: PITLOCHRY TO BRAEMAR & BLAIRGOWRIE

ALTITUDE: 1,121.90M	HEIGHT RANK: 33	OS GRID REFERENCE: NN971733

DATE .... TOTAL TIME ....

START TIME .... END TIME ....

DISTANCE .... STEPS ....

STARTING POINT ....

COMPANION(S) ....

....

WEATHER

TEMPERATURE
....
WIND ....

NOTE .... DIFFICULTY ☆☆☆☆☆

....
....
....
....
....

COUNTY: PERTH AND KINROSS

AN STUC

SECTION / REGION: 02B: GLEN LYON TO GLEN DOCHART & LOCH TAY

ALTITUDE: 1,117.10M   HEIGHT RANK: 36   OS GRID REFERENCE: NN638431

DATE .... TOTAL TIME ....

START TIME .... END TIME ....

DISTANCE .... STEPS ....

STARTING POINT ....

COMPANION(S) ....

....

WEATHER   TEMPERATURE .... WIND ....

NOTE .... DIFFICULTY ☆☆☆☆☆

....
....
....
....
....

COUNTY: PERTH AND KINROSS

BEINN GHLAS

SECTION / REGION: 02B: GLEN LYON TO GLEN DOCHART & LOCH TAY

| ALTITUDE: 1,103M | HEIGHT RANK: 48 | OS GRID REFERENCE: NN625404 |

DATE .... TOTAL TIME ....

START TIME .... END TIME ....

DISTANCE .... STEPS ....

STARTING POINT ....

COMPANION(S) ....

....

WEATHER

TEMPERATURE ....

WIND ....

NOTE .... DIFFICULTY ☆☆☆☆☆

....
....
....
....
....

COUNTY: PERTH AND KINROSS

SCHIEHALLION (SÌDH CHAILLEANN)

SECTION / REGION: 02A: LOCH RANNOCH TO GLEN LYON

| ALTITUDE: 1,083M | HEIGHT RANK: 59 | OS GRID REFERENCE: NN713547 |

DATE .... TOTAL TIME ....

START TIME .... END TIME ....

DISTANCE .... STEPS ....

STARTING POINT ....

COMPANION(S) ....

....

WEATHER

TEMPERATURE ....

WIND ....

NOTE .... DIFFICULTY ☆☆☆☆☆

....
....
....
....
....

COUNTY: PERTH AND KINROSS

BEINN A' CHREACHAIN

SECTION / REGION: 02A: LOCH RANNOCH TO GLEN LYON

ALTITUDE: 1,080.60M   HEIGHT RANK: 61   OS GRID REFERENCE: NN373440

DATE .... TOTAL TIME ....

START TIME .... END TIME ....

DISTANCE .... STEPS ....

STARTING POINT ....

COMPANION(S) ....

....

WEATHER

TEMPERATURE
....
WIND ....

NOTE .... DIFFICULTY ☆☆☆☆☆

....
....
....
....
....

COUNTY: PERTH AND KINROSS

BEINN HEASGARNICH

SECTION / REGION: 02B: GLEN LYON TO GLEN DOCHART & LOCH TAY

ALTITUDE: 1,077.40M   HEIGHT RANK: 63   OS GRID REFERENCE: NN413383

DATE .... TOTAL TIME ....

START TIME .... END TIME ....

DISTANCE .... STEPS ....

STARTING POINT ....

COMPANION(S) ....

....

WEATHER

TEMPERATURE
....
WIND ....

NOTE .... DIFFICULTY ☆☆☆☆☆

....
....
....
....
....

COUNTY: PERTH AND KINROSS

BEINN A' GHLÒ - BRÀIGH COIRE CHRUINN-BHALGAIN

SECTION / REGION: 06B: PITLOCHRY TO BRAEMAR & BLAIRGOWRIE

ALTITUDE: 1,070M   HEIGHT RANK: 66   OS GRID REFERENCE: NN945724

DATE .... TOTAL TIME ....

START TIME .... END TIME ....

DISTANCE .... STEPS ....

STARTING POINT ....

COMPANION(S) ....

....

WEATHER

TEMPERATURE
....
WIND ....

NOTE .... DIFFICULTY ☆☆☆☆☆

....
....
....
....
....

COUNTY: PERTH AND KINROSS

MEALL CORRANAICH

SECTION / REGION: 02B: GLEN LYON TO GLEN DOCHART & LOCH TAY

ALTITUDE: 1,069M	HEIGHT RANK: 68	OS GRID REFERENCE: NN615410

DATE .... TOTAL TIME ....

START TIME.................................. END TIME ....

DISTANCE................................... STEPS ....

STARTING POINT ....

COMPANION(S) ....

....

WEATHER

TEMPERATURE ....

WIND ....

NOTE .... DIFFICULTY ☆☆☆☆☆

....
....
....
....
....

COUNTY: PERTH AND KINROSS

GLAS TULAICHEAN

SECTION / REGION: 06B: PITLOCHRY TO BRAEMAR & BLAIRGOWRIE

ALTITUDE: 1,051M   HEIGHT RANK: 79   OS GRID REFERENCE: NO051760

DATE .... TOTAL TIME ....

START TIME .... END TIME ....

DISTANCE .... STEPS ....

STARTING POINT ....

COMPANION(S) ....

....

WEATHER

TEMPERATURE ....

WIND ....

NOTE .... DIFFICULTY ☆☆☆☆☆

....
....
....
....
....

COUNTY: PERTH AND KINROSS

MEALL NAN TARMACHAN

SECTION / REGION: 02B: GLEN LYON TO GLEN DOCHART & LOCH TAY

ALTITUDE: 1,043.60M   HEIGHT RANK: 90   OS GRID REFERENCE: NN585389

DATE .... TOTAL TIME ....

START TIME .... END TIME ....

DISTANCE .... STEPS ....

STARTING POINT ....

COMPANION(S) ....

....

WEATHER

TEMPERATURE ....

WIND ....

NOTE .... DIFFICULTY ☆☆☆☆☆

....
....
....
....
....

COUNTY: PERTH AND KINROSS

CÀRN MAIRG

SECTION / REGION: 02A: LOCH RANNOCH TO GLEN LYON

ALTITUDE: 1,042M   HEIGHT RANK: 91   OS GRID REFERENCE: NN684512

DATE .... TOTAL TIME ....

START TIME .... END TIME ....

DISTANCE .... STEPS ....

STARTING POINT ....

COMPANION(S) ....

....

WEATHER   TEMPERATURE
☀ ☁ ⛅ 🌧 ⛈ ❄   ....
● ● ● ● ● ●   WIND ....

NOTE .... DIFFICULTY ☆☆☆☆☆

....

....

....

....

....

COUNTY: PERTH AND KINROSS

CÀRN AN RÌGH

SECTION / REGION: 06B: PITLOCHRY TO BRAEMAR & BLAIRGOWRIE

ALTITUDE: 1,029M HEIGHT RANK: 102 OS GRID REFERENCE: NO028772

DATE .... TOTAL TIME ....

START TIME .... END TIME ....

DISTANCE .... STEPS ....

STARTING POINT ....

COMPANION(S) ....

....

WEATHER

TEMPERATURE
....
WIND ....

NOTE .... DIFFICULTY ☆☆☆☆☆

....
....
....
....
....

COUNTY: PERTH AND KINROSS

CÀRN GORM

SECTION / REGION: 02A: LOCH RANNOCH TO GLEN LYON

ALTITUDE: 1,029M   HEIGHT RANK: 103   OS GRID REFERENCE: NN635500

DATE .... TOTAL TIME ....

START TIME .... END TIME ....

DISTANCE .... STEPS ....

STARTING POINT ....

COMPANION(S) ....

....

WEATHER

TEMPERATURE ....

WIND ....

NOTE .... DIFFICULTY ☆☆☆☆☆

....

....

....

....

....

COUNTY: PERTH AND KINROSS

BEINN DEARG

SECTION / REGION: 06A: GLEN TROMIE TO GLEN TILT

ALTITUDE: 1,008.70M   HEIGHT RANK: 124   OS GRID REFERENCE: NN852778

DATE .... TOTAL TIME ....

START TIME .... END TIME ....

DISTANCE .... STEPS ....

STARTING POINT ....

COMPANION(S) ....

....

WEATHER

TEMPERATURE
....
WIND ....

NOTE .... DIFFICULTY ☆☆☆☆☆

....
....
....
....
....

COUNTY: PERTH AND KINROSS

MEALL GREIGH

SECTION / REGION: 02B: GLEN LYON TO GLEN DOCHART & LOCH TAY

ALTITUDE: 1,001M   HEIGHT RANK: 136   OS GRID REFERENCE: NN674438

DATE .... TOTAL TIME ....

START TIME .... END TIME ....

DISTANCE .... STEPS ....

STARTING POINT ....

COMPANION(S) ....

....

WEATHER

TEMPERATURE
....
WIND ....

NOTE .... DIFFICULTY ☆☆☆☆☆

....
....
....
....
....

COUNTY: PERTH AND KINROSS

SGAIRNEACH MHÒR

SECTION / REGION: 05A: LOCH ERICHT TO GLEN TROMIE & GLEN GARRY

| ALTITUDE: 991M | HEIGHT RANK: 155 | OS GRID REFERENCE: NN598731 |

DATE .... TOTAL TIME ....

START TIME .... END TIME ....

DISTANCE .... STEPS ....

STARTING POINT ....

COMPANION(S) ....

....

WEATHER

TEMPERATURE
....
WIND ....

NOTE .... DIFFICULTY ☆☆☆☆☆

....
....
....
....
....

COUNTY: PERTH AND KINROSS

BEN VORLICH

SECTION / REGION: 01B: STRATHYRE TO STRATHALLAN

ALTITUDE: 985.3M   HEIGHT RANK: 164   OS GRID REFERENCE: NN629189

DATE .... TOTAL TIME ....

START TIME .... END TIME ....

DISTANCE .... STEPS ....

STARTING POINT ....

COMPANION(S) ....

....

WEATHER

TEMPERATURE ....

WIND ....

NOTE .... DIFFICULTY ☆☆☆☆☆

....
....
....
....
....

COUNTY: PERTH AND KINROSS

MEALL NAN AIGHEAN

SECTION / REGION: 02A: LOCH RANNOCH TO GLEN LYON

ALTITUDE: 981M   HEIGHT RANK: 171   OS GRID REFERENCE: NN694496

DATE .... TOTAL TIME ....

START TIME .... END TIME ....

DISTANCE .... STEPS ....

STARTING POINT ....

COMPANION(S) ....

....

WEATHER

TEMPERATURE
....
WIND ....

NOTE .... DIFFICULTY ☆☆☆☆☆

....
....
....
....
....

COUNTY: PERTH AND KINROSS

BEINN A' GHLÒ - CÀRN LIATH

SECTION / REGION: 06B: PITLOCHRY TO BRAEMAR & BLAIRGOWRIE

ALTITUDE: 976M HEIGHT RANK: 179 OS GRID REFERENCE: NN936698

DATE .... TOTAL TIME ....

START TIME .... END TIME ....

DISTANCE .... STEPS ....

STARTING POINT ....

COMPANION(S) ....

....

WEATHER

TEMPERATURE ....

WIND ....

NOTE .... DIFFICULTY ☆☆☆☆☆

COUNTY: PERTH AND KINROSS

MEALL GARBH

SECTION / REGION: 02A: LOCH RANNOCH TO GLEN LYON

| ALTITUDE: 968M | HEIGHT RANK: 186 | OS GRID REFERENCE: NN647516 |

DATE .... TOTAL TIME ....

START TIME .... END TIME ....

DISTANCE .... STEPS ....

STARTING POINT ....

COMPANION(S) ....

....

WEATHER

TEMPERATURE
....

WIND ....

NOTE .... DIFFICULTY ☆☆☆☆☆

....

....

....

....

....

COUNTY: PERTH AND KINROSS

CÀRN A' CHLAMAIN

SECTION / REGION: 06A: GLEN TROMIE TO GLEN TILT

ALTITUDE: 963.5M   HEIGHT RANK: 192   OS GRID REFERENCE: NN915758

DATE .... TOTAL TIME ....

START TIME .... END TIME ....

DISTANCE .... STEPS ....

STARTING POINT ....

COMPANION(S) ....

....

WEATHER

TEMPERATURE ....

WIND ....

NOTE .... DIFFICULTY ☆☆☆☆☆

....
....
....
....
....

COUNTY: PERTH AND KINROSS

STUCHD AN LOCHAIN

SECTION / REGION: 02A: LOCH RANNOCH TO GLEN LYON

| ALTITUDE: 960M | HEIGHT RANK: 196 | OS GRID REFERENCE: NN483448 |

DATE .... TOTAL TIME ....

START TIME .... END TIME ....

DISTANCE .... STEPS ....

STARTING POINT ....

COMPANION(S) ....

....

WEATHER

TEMPERATURE ....

WIND ....

NOTE .... DIFFICULTY ☆☆☆☆☆

....
....
....
....
....

COUNTY: PERTH AND KINROSS

BEINN MHANACH

SECTION / REGION: 02A: LOCH RANNOCH TO GLEN LYON

ALTITUDE: 953M　　HEIGHT RANK: 211　　OS GRID REFERENCE: NN373411

DATE .... TOTAL TIME ....

START TIME .... END TIME ....

DISTANCE .... STEPS ....

STARTING POINT ....

COMPANION(S) ....

....

WEATHER

TEMPERATURE ....

WIND ....

NOTE .... DIFFICULTY ☆☆☆☆☆

....
....
....
....
....

COUNTY: PERTH AND KINROSS

MEALL BUIDHE

SECTION / REGION: 02A: LOCH RANNOCH TO GLEN LYON

| ALTITUDE: 932.1M | HEIGHT RANK: 248 | OS GRID REFERENCE: NN498499 |

DATE .... TOTAL TIME ....

START TIME .... END TIME ....

DISTANCE .... STEPS ....

STARTING POINT ....

COMPANION(S) ....

....

WEATHER

TEMPERATURE ....

WIND ....

NOTE .... DIFFICULTY ☆☆☆☆☆

....
....
....
....
....

COUNTY: PERTH AND KINROSS

BEN CHONZIE

SECTION / REGION: 01A: LOCH TAY TO PERTH

| ALTITUDE: 931M | HEIGHT RANK: 249 | OS GRID REFERENCE: NN773308 |

DATE .... TOTAL TIME ....

START TIME .... END TIME ....

DISTANCE .... STEPS ....

STARTING POINT ....

COMPANION(S) ....

....

WEATHER

TEMPERATURE ....

WIND ....

NOTE .... DIFFICULTY ☆☆☆☆☆

....
....
....
....
....

COUNTY: PERTH AND KINROSS

MEALL A' CHOIRE LEITH

SECTION / REGION: 02B: GLEN LYON TO GLEN DOCHART & LOCH TAY

| ALTITUDE: 925.6M | HEIGHT RANK: 263 | OS GRID REFERENCE: NN612438 |

DATE .... TOTAL TIME ....

START TIME .... END TIME ....

DISTANCE .... STEPS ....

STARTING POINT ....

COMPANION(S) ....

....

WEATHER

TEMPERATURE
....
WIND ....

NOTE .... DIFFICULTY ☆☆☆☆☆

....
....
....
....
....

COUNTY: PERTH AND KINROSS / STIRLING

CREAG MHÒR

SECTION / REGION: 02B: GLEN LYON TO GLEN DOCHART & LOCH TAY

ALTITUDE: 1,046.80M   HEIGHT RANK: 84   OS GRID REFERENCE: NN391361

DATE .... TOTAL TIME ....

START TIME .... END TIME ....

DISTANCE .... STEPS ....

STARTING POINT ....

COMPANION(S) ....

....

WEATHER

TEMPERATURE ....

WIND ....

NOTE .... DIFFICULTY ☆☆☆☆☆

....
....
....
....
....

COUNTY: PERTH AND KINROSS/ STIRLING

MEALL GHAORDAIDH

SECTION / REGION: 02B: GLEN LYON TO GLEN DOCHART & LOCH TAY

| ALTITUDE: 1,039.80M | HEIGHT RANK: 93 | OS GRID REFERENCE: NN514397 |

DATE .... TOTAL TIME ....

START TIME................................. END TIME ....

DISTANCE.................................... STEPS ....

STARTING POINT ....

COMPANION(S) ....

....

WEATHER

TEMPERATURE ....

WIND ....

NOTE .... DIFFICULTY ☆☆☆☆☆

....
....
....
....
....

COUNTY: PERTH AND KINROSS / STIRLING

STUC A' CHROIN

SECTION / REGION: 01B: STRATHYRE TO STRATHALLAN

| ALTITUDE: 973M | HEIGHT RANK: 184 | OS GRID REFERENCE: NN617174 |

DATE .... TOTAL TIME ....

START TIME .... END TIME ....

DISTANCE .... STEPS ....

STARTING POINT ....

COMPANION(S) ....

....

WEATHER

TEMPERATURE ....

WIND ....

NOTE .... DIFFICULTY ☆☆☆☆☆

....
....
....
....
....

COUNTY: STIRLING

BEN MORE (A' BHEINN MHÒR)

SECTION / REGION: 01C: LOCH LOMOND TO STRATHYRE

ALTITUDE: 1,174M   HEIGHT RANK: 16   OS GRID REFERENCE: NN432244

DATE .... TOTAL TIME ....

START TIME .... END TIME ....

DISTANCE .... STEPS ....

STARTING POINT ....

COMPANION(S) ....

....

WEATHER

TEMPERATURE ....

WIND ....

NOTE .... DIFFICULTY ☆☆☆☆☆

....

....

....

....

....

COUNTY: STIRLING

STOB BINNEIN

SECTION / REGION: 01C: LOCH LOMOND TO STRATHYRE

ALTITUDE: 1,165M HEIGHT RANK: 18 OS GRID REFERENCE: NN434227

DATE .... TOTAL TIME ....

START TIME .... END TIME ....

DISTANCE .... STEPS ....

STARTING POINT ....

COMPANION(S) ....

....

WEATHER

TEMPERATURE ....

WIND ....

NOTE .... DIFFICULTY ☆☆☆☆☆

....
....
....
....
....

COUNTY: STIRLING

BEN LUI (BEINN LAOIGH)

SECTION / REGION: 01D: INVERARAY TO CRIANLARICH

ALTITUDE: 1,131.40M   HEIGHT RANK: 27   OS GRID REFERENCE: NN266262

DATE .... TOTAL TIME ....

START TIME .... END TIME ....

DISTANCE .... STEPS ....

STARTING POINT ....

COMPANION(S) ....

....

WEATHER

TEMPERATURE
....
WIND ....

NOTE .... DIFFICULTY ☆☆☆☆☆

....
....
....
....
....

COUNTY: STIRLING

CRUACH ARDRAIN

SECTION / REGION: 01C: LOCH LOMOND TO STRATHYRE

ALTITUDE: 1,045.90M   HEIGHT RANK: 87   OS GRID REFERENCE: NN409212

DATE .... TOTAL TIME ....

START TIME .... END TIME ....

DISTANCE .... STEPS ....

STARTING POINT ....

COMPANION(S) ....

....

WEATHER

TEMPERATURE ....

WIND ....

NOTE .... DIFFICULTY ☆☆☆☆☆

....

....

....

....

....

COUNTY: STIRLING

BEN OSS

SECTION / REGION: 01D: INVERARAY TO CRIANLARICH

| ALTITUDE: 1,029M | HEIGHT RANK: 101 | OS GRID REFERENCE: NN287253 |

DATE .... TOTAL TIME ....

START TIME .... END TIME ....

DISTANCE .... STEPS ....

STARTING POINT ....

COMPANION(S) ....

....

WEATHER

TEMPERATURE ....

WIND ....

NOTE .... DIFFICULTY ☆☆☆☆☆

COUNTY: STIRLING

BEINN CHALLUIM (BEN CHALLUM)

SECTION / REGION: 02B: GLEN LYON TO GLEN DOCHART & LOCH TAY

| ALTITUDE: 1,025M | HEIGHT RANK: 106 | OS GRID REFERENCE: NN386322 |

DATE .... TOTAL TIME ....

START TIME .... END TIME ....

DISTANCE .... STEPS ....

STARTING POINT ....

COMPANION(S) ....

....

WEATHER

TEMPERATURE ....

WIND ....

NOTE .... DIFFICULTY ☆☆☆☆☆

....
....
....
....
....

COUNTY: STIRLING

AN CAISTEAL

SECTION / REGION: 01C: LOCH LOMOND TO STRATHYRE

ALTITUDE: 995.9M HEIGHT RANK: 147 OS GRID REFERENCE: NN378193

DATE .... TOTAL TIME ....

START TIME .... END TIME ....

DISTANCE .... STEPS ....

STARTING POINT ....

COMPANION(S) ....

....

WEATHER

TEMPERATURE ....

WIND ....

NOTE .... DIFFICULTY ☆☆☆☆☆

....
....
....
....
....

COUNTY: STIRLING

BEINN DUBHCHRAIG

SECTION / REGION: 01D: INVERARAY TO CRIANLARICH

ALTITUDE: 978M HEIGHT RANK: 175 OS GRID REFERENCE: NN307254

DATE .... TOTAL TIME ....

START TIME .... END TIME ....

DISTANCE .... STEPS ....

STARTING POINT ....

COMPANION(S) ....

....

WEATHER

TEMPERATURE ....

WIND ....

NOTE .... DIFFICULTY ☆☆☆☆☆

....
....
....
....
....

COUNTY: STIRLING

BEN LOMOND (BEINN LAOMAINN)

SECTION / REGION: 01C: LOCH LOMOND TO STRATHYRE

ALTITUDE: 973.7M   HEIGHT RANK: 182   OS GRID REFERENCE: NN367028

DATE .... TOTAL TIME ....

START TIME .... END TIME ....

DISTANCE .... STEPS ....

STARTING POINT ....

COMPANION(S) ....

....

WEATHER

TEMPERATURE ....

WIND ....

NOTE .... DIFFICULTY ☆☆☆☆☆

....
....
....
....
....

COUNTY: STIRLING

MEALL GLAS

SECTION / REGION: 02B: GLEN LYON TO GLEN DOCHART & LOCH TAY

ALTITUDE: 959.3M   HEIGHT RANK: 198   OS GRID REFERENCE: NN431321

DATE .... TOTAL TIME ....

START TIME .... END TIME ....

DISTANCE .... STEPS ....

STARTING POINT ....

COMPANION(S) ....

....

WEATHER

TEMPERATURE ....

WIND ....

NOTE .... DIFFICULTY ☆☆☆☆☆

....
....
....
....
....

COUNTY: STIRLING

BEINN TULAICHEAN

SECTION / REGION: 01C: LOCH LOMOND TO STRATHYRE

ALTITUDE: 945.8M　　HEIGHT RANK: 222　　OS GRID REFERENCE: NN416196

DATE .... TOTAL TIME ....

START TIME .... END TIME ....

DISTANCE .... STEPS ....

STARTING POINT ....

COMPANION(S) ....

....

WEATHER

TEMPERATURE ....

WIND ....

NOTE .... DIFFICULTY ☆☆☆☆☆

....

....

....

....

....

COUNTY: STIRLING

BEINN A' CHROIN

SECTION / REGION: 01C: LOCH LOMOND TO STRATHYRE

ALTITUDE: 941.4M   HEIGHT RANK: 231   OS GRID REFERENCE: NN387185

DATE .... TOTAL TIME ....

START TIME .... END TIME ....

DISTANCE .... STEPS ....

STARTING POINT ....

COMPANION(S) ....

....

WEATHER

TEMPERATURE ....

WIND ....

NOTE .... DIFFICULTY ☆☆☆☆☆

....

....

....

....

....

COUNTY: STIRLING

BEINN CHABHAIR

SECTION / REGION: 01C: LOCH LOMOND TO STRATHYRE

ALTITUDE: 932.2M　　HEIGHT RANK: 247　　OS GRID REFERENCE: NN367179

DATE .... TOTAL TIME ....

START TIME .... END TIME ....

DISTANCE .... STEPS ....

STARTING POINT ....

COMPANION(S) ....

....

WEATHER

TEMPERATURE ....

WIND ....

NOTE .... DIFFICULTY ☆☆☆☆☆

....
....
....
....
....

COUNTY: STIRLING

SGIATH CHUIL

SECTION / REGION: 02B: GLEN LYON TO GLEN DOCHART & LOCH TAY

ALTITUDE: 920.1M   HEIGHT RANK: 270   OS GRID REFERENCE: NN462317

DATE .... TOTAL TIME ....

START TIME .... END TIME ....

DISTANCE .... STEPS ....

STARTING POINT ....

COMPANION(S) ....

....

WEATHER

TEMPERATURE ....

WIND ....

NOTE .... DIFFICULTY ☆☆☆☆☆

....
....
....
....
....

Notes

Printed in Great Britain
by Amazon